Praise for *ReRoot*

A profoundly engaging, wise, and timely book inviting readers to become part of a process of reconnection with Nature through the intelligence of trees. The need to redefine the predominant relationship with the natural world is now imperative and the author shows a path to healing and wholeness—I loved it!

—David Lorimer
Programme Director of the Scientific
and Medical Network
UK

We are suffering from separation sickness, a global connection crisis. This book is so helpful in orientating and guiding us into the deep and necessary work of re-weaving ourselves back into the web of life.

—Mary-Jayne Rust
Ecopsychologist, Jungian Analyst, Author
London

This magical book invites us into a journey to let go of all that divides us and discover instead the beauty in our interconnectedness. It's playful, profound, wise, and unconventional—a must read for anyone who believes it's time to awaken our collective imagination.

—Radha Ruparell
Author of *Brave Now*

Louise Marra has a deeply profound, playful and poetic way to take you on a journey to reconnect with the web of life, our deepest wisdom, and power, through befriending trees. Connecting with trees has been one of the most transformative experiences of my life and *ReRoot* has been a precious guide in deepening this journey. This work is so needed in our time and a gift to humanity. I especially hope all changemakers embrace the opportunity to engage in this movement.

–Shruthi Vijayakumar
Young Global Shaper

Louise Marra's *ReRoot* is a subtle, enchanting, and powerful guide to re-membering our undividedness from nature–in relationship with the trees that give us life. Rooted in the knowledge systems of her Māori ancestry, of the *Ngāi Tūhoe* people, Marra takes the reader into deep relationship, a relationship that is already there but forgotten by us humans. Healing happens through wholeness, a wisdom that Marra offers.

–Dr. Elizabeth Debold
Author, Founder, *One World of Dialogue*
Editor, *evolve* Magazine, *evolve* World

Come home to body, to soil, to tree, to planet. We can only respond to our world once we fully land and take our place in the midst of all creation. Louise Marra invites us to arrive into the fullness of who we have always been.

–Kosha Joubert
CEO Pocket Project

It's a bold ask to invite the world to love and relate with trees intimately, and yet only bold asks have changed our lives and our world around us.

Louise challenges us to look beyond our own boundaries to create a new meaning of "becoming whole again," and she is entitled to ask that question as she walked the journey herself.

It's a new way and a bold way, an olive branch extraordinaire and so deeply needed in our segregated world.

ReRoot and becoming intimate with a tree is an invitation to becoming intimate with yourself again. Do you accept the challenge by doing what you're about to read in this magical book? Only reading isn't helping your health or humanity and nature. We need you to do it!

Let's walk with Louise side by side on the journey deeper into the forest of trees. Take her trusting hand and walk into every chapter, falling deeper and deeper in love with your trees.

–Paul Zonneveld
Author of *EMERGENT: The Power of Systemic Intelligence to Navigate the Complexity of M & A*

ReRoot

the nature of change
through the system of trees

LOUISE MARRA

Edited by Laurie Knight

Cover Design by Kristina Edstrom

EMP⊙WER
P   R   E   S   S

An Imprint for GracePoint Publishing (www.GracePointPublishing.com)

GracePoint Matrix, LLC
624 S. Cascade Ave, Suite 201
Colorado Springs, CO 80903
www.GracePointMatrix.com
Email: Admin@GracePointMatrix.com
SAN # 991-6032

A Library of Congress Control Number has been requested and is pending.

ISBN: (Paperback) 978-1-955272-50-6

eISBN: 978-1-955272-51-3

Books may be purchased for educational, business, or sales promotional use.
For bulk order requests and price schedule contact:
Orders@GracePointPublishing.com

Table of Contents

Dedication to the Reader

Malidoma Patrice Somé: What frequency have I lost that I cannot hear the tree speak?

My intent for this book is that we together deepen our understanding and practice as human beings of the alchemical art of photosynthesis, embodying light into aliveness and breath. May we open our subtle body systems to experience our connected self and together begin to restore with, and as the planet by re-breathing and rerooting health, vitality, and potential into all our natural systems of which we, as humans, are simply part of.

Foreword

The joy and the wonder that you will experience as you travel along, the journey amongst these pages is a blessing for us all, it will leave you changed and walking amongst the trees with a renewed hope and awe. Louise has unwound the mystery of communing with trees and the many gifts the journey opens within you along the way. As we awaken our senses to reengage with our multi-sensory abilities our desire to connect and commune with nature will heighten and welcome us back to ourselves, unity.

The invitation to come as you are, no judgement, no demands, or prework needed is refreshing and offers a safe place to drop all the things you think you know and begin the journey to opening your multi-sensory way of being in the world. My personal journey of co-creating with nature started a few years ago and I am beyond excited to be on this journey into relating with trees.

As I entered our forest here at Ubuntu, in the Green Mountains of Vermont, I was filled with excitement, nerves and the anticipation of meeting a new friend. As I walked with open eyes, I could feel my heart beating and my nerves all at full alert. It felt as if I was in a place where time and space collapsed and all that was left was the sound and motion of my feet pressing down on the forest floor with a tentative repetition. The crunch of leaves and twigs answering back with each footstep. From nowhere the wind moved by me as though a friend just passed. The wind is always an energy I experience great respect for and often when she shows up from what feels like nowhere (storm cell etc.) my body responds with going to my knees and this was no different. Without much conscious awareness I embraced the moment and simply sat back into it, not feeling an urge to get back on my feet. A ray of sunshine caught my attention, as it has been rainy here the past few weeks. As eyes followed the ray, I was seeing on the forest floor next to me to the heavens. I witnessed the most beautiful canopy above me. A deep and reverent knowing came across me as I slowly turned my head in the realisation that I was about to embark on a journey that would take me places that I could not even begin to imagine. I slowly turned to my side, and with a very open heart and a smile that consumed my whole face, introduced myself to my new tree friend.

It is with the deepest of gratitude and love that I thank Louise for bringing this beautiful work to life for us all, to my new "tree" friend for the adventures to come, and to you my friends that are reading this as you will be adding to the web of interconnected life as you so gracefully dissolve on this beautiful and divine journey.

–Alexsys Thompson
Author of *The Gratitude 540 Journal* series
and *The Power of a Graceful Leader*

The Invitation

I bring this book in a time of crisis and potential collapse because I am aware that many want to truly connect with nature and do not know how. My aim is to share some simple, practical, and profound ways to experiment with deepening your relationship with nature, yourself, and the amazing flows and rivers of life. I invite you to play, explore, connect, and have fun as you journey with me through these pages.

You see, humanity and the planet are at a crossroads in their relationship. It is the relationship that must be reset first and then together we may find solutions to the way forward. Without that, we may continue repeating the patterns of disconnect within the solutions, and nothing will change.

Restoration will only come through connection.

Connection and relationship are synonymous. If we stay in connection, we can stay relating—to ourselves, each other, the space between us, and the flow of nature. We are always affected and impacted by our connections, and we affect them; together we are co-relating and co-creating each moment. It is just that we have stopped feeling these connective threads and believe that we exist in isolation. Until we as humans can see and perceive that everyone around us, our situations, and our environment—especially nature—are all in relationship with each other and that our thoughts, actions, beliefs, and so forth affect each other, we will remain in a place of disconnect, and we will remain mired in old systems.

Disconnected people and systems will always create more disconnect. Disconnect has become a wide-spread disease, now wired into how our systems work and how we make decisions or offer solutions. Often fuelled by superiority, survival energy, fear, and trauma, we have found ourselves in a world that is orientated around humans being separate entities and not an intrinsic part of the natural systems we need to live in.

Separation itself is one of the primary traumas we all face. We cannot be well as individuals within an unwell world. Trauma isolates, and when isolated as humanity from the web of life and from each other, it means trauma leads the way, leads the solutions, unconsciously. We then stay on trauma highways and our solutions are from this unhealthy place. We need our connected selves to lead the solutions, but many lack the confidence, skills, and even the belief that it is possible.

While we have movements toward healing both our personal and collective traumas within our physical bodies and our planet, these are seen as separate issues. They are not. The relationship is the core issue; the *disconnect* is a core collective trauma we must now face together and resew ourselves back into the web of life.

Separation is a withdrawing, a pulling away, but it is a process not a reality. The pursuit of rugged individualism pioneered around the planet is something we have agreed to, colluded with. We are not separate; we need each other and nature to heal and feel whole.

We must now reverse this process of separating and begin a new movement of connection. This is the sacred act of rethreading and weaving ourselves back into relationship as an intrinsic part of nature's flow and apparatus.

This book is an invitation to voyage into this process of resetting our relationships and knitting ourselves back into the web of life. It is something we can all do. It is a beckoning into a way of seeing and being in the world that is unashamedly different from the dominant orthodoxies we mostly live by today. These are primarily based on extracting, using, consuming, discarding, and certainly taking for granted.

You may have resistances, denials, and protections of the systems by which you identify or the processes that you grew up believing to be true. No matter. Bring them all along and come anyway. Or you may read these words and think—no, feel, deep within—that there are resounding truths bubbling beneath and between these pages. Bring that too, and come along.

It is a transmuting book, a restorative and healing book. When we transmute, we take something and help to elevate or lift it to a higher level. This book may transmute you, or you may take the essence, apply it to your life, and rise higher in thought, in consciousness. You may feel restored, like a remembering has happened which urges you to reconnect and feel your way back. This book may incite healing as you journey through its pages. It is also a process, one we can all add to; it is not by any means complete. You will help complete it. Consider it a work in progress that you will all add your brilliance—your specific threads—to, which I hope to gather as we journey together. This will add to the creation of a forest of humans and trees, a new nest we build cooperatively, and the body of knowledge we need to develop a living and lived science of nature connection.

So dear reader, I implore you to give this a go. Please know it truly matters. If you reconnect yourself (and I daresay *with* yourself), the old-world western order of separation will get disrupted, and something mystical will happen for you and your whole family system in that one radical act of terminating the forward movement of separation, turning around, and sewing that thread of connection. Change happens once you refuse to follow the disconnected movement anymore. One rethreading creates a connection, creates a weave in a new tapestry, a new universal neural pattern. We become like the birds building a collective nest that we all get to live in.

Let us build together our re-embodiment and understanding of the living science of nature connection.

Come join me on this awkward, rewarding, frustrating, confusing, often disruptive journey that will rewire your brain and nervous system and while you do that, it will help create a new wiring for us all.

I will do my best to guide from my deepest integrity and my own experience of the richness of this type of contemplative and connective journey that takes us back into unity consciousness.

I am not an expert in trees. I am a relationist, and my aim is to take you into the relating realm.

I have written this book largely for a western orthodox world. I don't mean to exclude anyone. It is where I see the biggest reorientation and changes are needed.

For me, recovery of my roots has been—and still is—a long journey. Many in the world have mule blood rivers in them which I call *braided rivers*. Consider the weaving of your own heritage. Besides a blending of your birth parents, consider the origin of your deep, far-removed ancestors. If we embrace and immerse in some of these deep rivers, we can revolutionise our ways of knowing.

The mainstream world we seem to be "rivering" (living and flowing) in, is so good at assimilating. We need to undo a lot and that means within as well as without. Let this help undo the parts of your knowledge and map making that needs some reorientating.

Also, if, like me, you are recovering and deepening your indigenous roots, exploring those blood rivers within, then come along and this process can help you "reroot" yourself within your own safe space to then find your holistic, interconnected self again.

Not everything in this book is going to make sense to you on first reading. It is part of this evolution of thinking. Read it with breath, pausing when something doesn't make sense. Allow it to land without striving to understand. Please don't try to read this book from start to finish like a normal book. It may not make sense that way and more importantly, it could put you into overwhelm. We may all feel overwhelmed by nature, or by what we have done as humans to each other and by how far we have separated ourselves from nature and our natural current of life.

This book is not theoretical, it is a sewing, a threading, a weaving book, and it will resew you, fibre by yarn, one exercise at a time. Warning: You will need to learn to slow down, to do this work. Sewing nests is slow work.

This act of slowing is essential these days, to re-learn. Be patient as you recover this. It is a *joining* process to help you re-bond to the earth, your ground of being. It is something that needs slow building as it has been interrupted for most of us in our modern world. Many of us know, sense, or feel an interruption, a disconnection, but know not what to do about it. Others want to commune with nature, but no one wants to slow, convinced as they are that the current trajectory cannot be punctuated. We must endure the discomfort of slowing down as the practices within the book will explain.

We need to move from trying to solve a problem to weaving a new house, a nest, we can all live in.

Introduction

This book has found you.

It is a book that finds people. On some level you chose it; more importantly, it has chosen you.

And so, begins a simple, natural, exhilarating journey that takes you into the true flow of your being—your connected self, your interbeing—and back into the life-enhancing natural flow.

This may seem a small book, but it is a radically expansive process for you and for all of us. It is about rerooting yourself *into* yourself, your own body, and into the web of life by making a life-long friend, one you can relate and communicate with, breathe with, ask for advice from, lean on, heal with, expand with, and that you can give and receive love with.

There are things missing about us as humans. Overall, we have many challenges in our relationships, families, communities, and workplaces where we all struggle to create the deep layers of connection that allows for full human potential to flourish. This process of knitting ourselves back into the earth may seem youthful, immature, or even silly to some, but I invite you to explore, nonetheless.

Trees are vital to the whole planetary system we belong to. Trees are the lungs of the Earth. What we have done and are doing to our forests and all they provide is wrong on all levels. This vital relationship between humans and trees may well relieve our environmental crisis, creating healing within self, within groups, throughout humanity, and with the planet.

A relationship with a tree can reroot you, help you bond with the currents of life and help you reroot humanity in this time where humans are so unrooted, split, splintered, removed, cut off, disconnected, and lonely in separation. It is time to come back, to return into true connectedness for ourselves, each other, and for our wondrous planet.

This book is not about personifying trees, it is about "tree-ifying" you and us all, together. This is the magic we will weave as we find our true and tree selves.

The more of us that can connect in this way, the greater our chances for turning things around, and for returning to a healthier and more harmonious environment. Once we establish a connection, we can recreate a global forest, one that is an intricate dance between trees and humans that will help us create new, connected solutions that can heal our world.

Chapter 1
My Personal Story

I want to share a bit of how I know this is a worthwhile journey and why I offer it to the world now, with all my vulnerability, clarity, and in the spirit of being a continuous experimenter and learner.

A collision of layers within me, from the prosaic to the profound, has brought this book into being.

I grew up in remote Aotearoa, New Zealand, on a farm at the edge of the mystical *whenua* (land) and *ngahere* (forests) of the *Ngāi Tūhoe* tribe, *Te Urewera*. This beautiful place of the Children of the Mist, the Tūhoe people, is hard to describe in its essence: the emerald water "riverings" (river systems) are beings themselves; the trees are immense and magical (I have seen them light up in the middle of the night); the mountains overlook earth and sky as guardians, seeming to belong to both realms. There are many energies that come together in this place, yet they are held and threaded with the warm and potent grounding of Mother Earth. These are all in my veins, my own valleys, rivers, and mountains inside me. Often, I travel to these mystical deep cool rivers and light-filled trees of my first belonging. They are always available to me, in me, especially the tree friends I made.

As I strode into life and many big roles, these trees and rivers remained my friends, and I came and went from them. One night, many years ago, I had a vivid dream where my mother (Joan), grandmother (Hihiria, Cis), great grandmother (Ani), and great, great grandmother (Motoi) were all in a line, pointing to an opening in a huge tree's trunk, "Go in, go in," they said. "Go in here, we will help guide you. You must go in."

So, I did, and this book represents my own winding path of "going in." This going in was both going into a deeper relationship with the natural world and going into my own body system, into my own true nature, heart, and authenticity. It was also a process of discovery into the trauma and horror of colonisation and its swirling current effects on us. It was seeing into my interbeing, my interdependence, and recovering my natural bonding process, my ability to relate intimately, and not through layers of walls, bracing, and protection. Bringing myself out of the dominant orthodoxy and awakening back into the web of life, into my place in the constellation of life I learnt—and am still learning—how to reroot.

I worked for many years in the environmental movement, starting nearly forty years ago as an activist and then working with leaders and changemakers in NGOs, government, private sector, and philanthropy, on how they change systems. I saw that much of the environmental work was being done without the Earth, without the connection to earth. All done by human effort, huge human effort, yet *disconnected* human effort.

"Nothing for me without me," Mother Earth said to me in a meditation.

It has taken me years to be so confident that this con-nection back to earth, as earth, is in fact, primary and foundational work. I realised how important this reconnective work is, and how much I truly believe we will not solve the problems of our world without it. I do not wobble on this. Disconnected people will keep coming up with disconnected solutions that won't work as they come from a trauma source and continue that trauma highway into the world, all with good intent.

These trauma highways have led to the horror of where we have arrived as a human species. I believe in the magnificence and intrinsic wholeness of our true nature as humans and what a symphony we *could* be.

And we are not.

Often.

This.

We must build our capacity to be with the horror of what we have caused, been complicit with, mute in, and numbed out from if we are to create a world where all can thrive. There is much written about the current horror of environmental collapse we are in. This book is not focused on describing those, but on creating a new relatedness that can face and feel them together. You will see more and feel more of the horrors we have created as you wake up in this process to your inherent relatedness to the natural world.

As we open our hearts and the tendrils of our being back into our interbeing, we turn ourselves back on and start to feel as a species what we have done but with new inner resources to help face it and feel it.

In meeting the horror and the magnificence of us, together we may map-make a connected future where ubiquitous human superiority can be restored into mutual connectivity.

Seeing my distortions–the trauma wounds, the disruption in my own rhythm, and the disorganised system within me– helped me see how I needed to and could rewire and repair the way I "system" from my own being. I emanated what I was trying to change. This fuelled my own awakening journey into wholeness, into seeing energy currents and patterns, and into the delicate, sensitive, and delicious nature of my sensing body. Our nervous systems have sensory antennas constantly picking up signals and attuning back into nature's signals and vibrations. This affects and heightens our own *mauri*, life force. I recognised and realised that I must reclaim my body, re-join with it–as part of the journey of relating back to nature. You see, our bodies *are* nature, they are Mother Earth. Your bodies are the most intimate relationship with nature you can have.

I think of myself as a braided river. I have many ancestral lines that come together in my body. I am indigenous to this land of *Aotearoa* (Māori for New Zealand) being part of the *Ngāi Tūhoe* tribe, and I also have many other rivers: Scottish, Irish, French, Italian, English. I am both colonised and coloniser and much of my life has been trying to bring these rivers together within me and outside of me.

This book draws on all the rivers in my being and is guided by the ancestors in my lines; my Māori and Celtic ancestors have been the most active, the most vocal. It also draws on the direct whispers that came to me during dreams, while writing under my tree, from my tree friends, while meditating, or while just doing the dishes. These whispers come directly and profoundly.

The native language of New Zealand, *Te Reo Māori*, comes from the land, the earth, as indigenous languages do. The *reo* has so many portal words, words that cannot be translated directly into English. I will use *te reo* terms throughout the book as an invitation into a portal that can take you further and deeper. They require you to travel with these words, walk with them, often for years. They invite you into deep ways of being and seeing. Indigenous languages like *te reo* often are also bridges into the natural world, coming from sounds that resonate to the beings, such as tree beings of the land. A glossary of terms is at the back of the book. Enjoy and savour the taste and feel of these words in your mouth as you open to them. They are beautiful, potent, powerful, and they point to deep truths about life.

Chapter 2
The Science of Falling in Love with Life

Understanding a little about the autonomic nervous system will be helpful in this journey of weaving. It holds many clues for us of where to head next and the amazing bodies of work being done to connect us to our somatic selves, our full body system, and not just our minds, which is part of the key to this book.

Polyvagal theory, the work by Stephen Porges and others, is seen as the science of falling in love with life. Isn't that beautiful? As this journey is about a love affair with nature and life, it is very relevant for us as we walk this path.

There are two major parts to the nervous system, the sympathetic and the parasympathetic. The sympathetic system is best described as our "on" system, where we are activated and ready to spring into action, and the parasympathetic is more of our rest and recovery or "off" system. The parasympathetic has two parts, the ventral vagal and the dorsal vagal (or front and back), each with very different effects on the body.

Understanding how these operate and how we navigate them heavily shapes the way we experience ourselves and our life. The more we can understand and be aware of our nervous system, the more we can regulate ourselves and receive more life. We may also be a regulating resource for those around us, as it is proven that our very presence affects those in close proximity. It heavily influences our ability to be present with more of who we are and more of the natural world and natural currents we are part of and are part of us.

We are born with an underdeveloped parasympathetic system which matures in sync with our primary caregiver. We co-regulated with them, and with practise, learnt (or failed to learn) how to regulate ourselves through neuroception, our mirror neurons, and soothing/self-soothing practices (like rocking, tactile stimulation like rubbing or thumb-sucking, cranial nerve activation, etc.).

We need to learn how to navigate ourselves and our autonomic responses. We are complex beings and many of our responses arise unconsciously. As this journey is entirely about navigation, this understanding of our nervous system has helped shape this book.

I studied the groundbreaking work of Peter Levine and Porges in Somatic Experiencing, which has helped me connect with myself and nature in increasing beautiful depths. I discovered and recovered parts of myself I had divorced from, either consciously or unconsciously, and found healthier and more resourced ways to be with the complexity of myself. My connection with trees has been an enormous resource in this process.

I interpret for myself that the ventral vagal state is a place of interbeing and interdependence; it is our prime place of connection. (Stephen Porges refers to this as the social engagement system within his Polyvagal Theory.) When we are in our optimal state as humans, we are alert, open, curious, spacious, and ready for connection with ourselves, other humans, and of course all the world around us. We are not ruled by strategies we developed for safety, so we can open to connect. We are naturally and authentically being us, and not trying to be anyone else which is why we are open and curious about others and wanting to experience life in fuller terms with and via others.

When we are in our sympathetic systems, we are in a contracted state, in fight or flight and in competition with others around us, including the natural world. We see others—and possibly everything around us—as a threat. Consider to what extent you recognise this state in the world and within. The hard part is that most of what triggers us into this state is from the past, not the present. The good part is this is not arising to blindside us, but to be healed, to pendulate out of our bodies which have stored past overwhelm and trauma, so we can get more space and aliveness. We need to work with these activations to change and grow, not to stifle them. They are all intelligent and playing an amazing role in our body systems. We can learn to see these activations as one of the biggest adventures of our life!

Our dorsal state, part of the parasympathetic, brings immobilisation. It is so clever. It is the numbing and shut down of our system when things get (or got) too much.

Trauma not only comes from distinct events, but it is also caused by the many times where anything was too much, too soon, too early, and we were too alone to feel and cope with it. The body system stored it for later when there is or was enough support to process it.

How we work with these parts of our system is the biggest adventure of our life (or we need to see it that way or we are in for a great war within ourselves). We can end up in a real battle of protection and survival and this may conflict with our yearning for intimacy and connection. We can spend our life caught between these and never really learn, grow, change, connect, and be in the fluidity of our evolving beingness.

We need to resource and re-source ourselves and almost retrain and rewire our system to know how to come back into the ventral vagal. When we are out of it, our body and brain have been hijacked and held in survival and deep fear responses!

Most of what happens in the nervous system occurs suddenly beneath our conscious awareness; we may experience a trigger, an activation, with little warning, because our nervous system sensed something that reminded it of the past threat. It was encoded or wired into us with a chemical signature, alerting us to danger. We often have no memory of an event, but the resurgence of a chemical imprint may cause us to feel sudden anxiety, fear, or dread. We need to build our resources and our awareness to discern what is happening in the present and what is arriving to be healed and evolved from the past.

In this book you will develop resources for yourself to be able to help navigate your nervous system. It will help you find your way back to a supported ventral vagal state and thereby return to your natural intimacy with life. It will help you develop more choice for connection and away from fear and survival, all through your reconnection to your interbeing *with* and *as* the web of life.

Again, I am interested in this for you, and I am vitally interested in this for us. This book is a movement from our connected place, our ventral vagal, the only place we can truly connect and the only place we can truly "world" anew from. We cannot keep following the collective sympathetic movement of fear, protection, and survival that has kept us transferring the trauma from generation to generation. It is time for restoration.

This is the nest building, the human-tree foresting. We all take responsibility to grow our capacity to come back into this place in ourselves, which is back into the fabric of connected life. Then these new threads create *whāriki*, woven mats, that make it possible for the fresh and connected solutions to arrive. It can help us transmute and transform the past trauma energies, so we don't continue the old trauma highways of the past and continue pain-inducing behaviours onto each other and into our already tenuous future.

Here, this process is helping those up for the journey to become part of this connected movement as a radical step of active change. The change is in the connection, and the connection reorients the timeline of our collective future.

As I have said, this relating and connecting is not meant to be a struggle. I really don't want you to work hard. My wish for you is all in the yielding. Without yielding and feeling, you won't detect or sense the simple and subtle communication of nature with us.

Less, less. Effort creates tension; tension creates contraction; contraction creates less availability of yourself for feeling. Working hard reduces the ability to learn and feel the great symphony of our systems inside, always talking to us, always responding to the outside world, to nature.

Yielding is a process, and there is so much yielding needed; it is vital to the healing of ourselves and our planet.

We are also going to practice attending. We are always attending to something. Sadly, in general, attending to nature and its flow has not been what we as humans have been doing.

We must.

Our attention now needs to go to this flow of life; we need to catch these currents and natural pathways and flow with them. All natural systems, including our own, are in support of health, optimisation of energy, and flow. If we pay attention to the coherence and harmony trying to emerge, I believe it grows.

I don't think we need to rescue nature; we all have self-healing mechanisms within us, just as the Earth has its own self-healing mechanism, and we need to come back into coherence, into flow, for us to follow these natural beautiful currents.

We all want to be rid of the horrible feelings of tension inside. We cannot get rid of them, for where will we put them? There is no *out there*. We can integrate and turn them into flow. This is the real work. The only way out is in.

You have some tension to turn back into flow and I also have some. The nervous system work helps us be able to navigate this to slowly come back into connection. We are good at giving all our attention to what is not working on both the inside and outside and creating many problems from this attention. In these processes they have also invited our attention into the emergent flow of life trying to correct and harmonise *itself.*

The body symphony knows how to sing. Your body systems know this; they know nature language. It is a great relaxation that creates the most authentic *waiata*, or song. I know this takes time to believe but more importantly to feel and trust.

So much is in our breath. We take for granted that which flows so effortlessly from that moment of entry in this world right up until the final breath. Breath is life, yet we don't often pay attention unless we have been compromised. Notice your own breath now. The inhale to create freshness, the exhale to yield. Focus on your exhale to yield and settle your *mauri*, life force, and come into a state of *mauri tau*, relaxation. The more you get to know this place the more you will sing your song in the world.

Chapter 3
What on Earth is the Global Human-Tree Forest?

Now that the nervous system has been introduced, let's venture into our collective nervous system and how this might enable us to create a different future.

First, don't try too hard to grasp it; the mind will interfere and be derogatory about it. Don't believe the mind around this; come into your heart and into a paradigm I and many others already inhabit, one where everything is energy.

I will try and lead you through this as logically as possible, within this paradigm.

There is no doubt that in the dominant orthodox world, people are considered (and act as if they are) separate from nature. We then become hyper-individualistic with no connective tissue in our ways of being creating disparity between the goals we set for ourselves and the impact these have on the inner and outer world.

This means we *feel* separate but also that there is a *process* of distancing from nature, so our experience of ourselves feels like it is other (i.e., there is me and there is nature).

We form a protective shield and a bracing in us that becomes like a structure in our body systems, in our being, that keeps us from being intimate with others and nature. The shield inhibits the natural bonding process. This protective shield or shell is highly intelligent; it helps us feel safe and, in some ways, contained.

It also keeps us isolated. Separate.

From that collective act of separating, because we keep doing it, we end up as isolated units trying to come up with connected solutions, but that is not possible. Separate people living isolated, independent lives cannot truly create connected solutions. We must connect to create what will work to elevate all of humankind.

Let us all connect and then solution-make.

To connect, we need to sew back threads of connectivity, sew them right through that protective layer in us and into the web of life—nature—so that thread can grow and nourish a connective tissue, a fabric of vibrant threads between us. It has become frayed and unravelled over time, but it's time to heal. It is time to create a healing movement that turns around this connection crisis.

Trees are available for relating, for this connection. They are connected, networked beings themselves; they have systems we can relate to easily. Their intelligence and abilities to relate are still being discovered but you can find this out for yourself, be part of this science of nature connection of human-tree forest building.

As we go through this process, it is about you sewing and weaving these threads; imagine their colour and texture as you relate through this separate and protective layer.

What if you begin with connecting to yourself in an authentic and new way, as a full part of nature, and then you find a tree to connect with to begin this process of rethreading in a felt way, a relational way? We cannot reconnect by only thinking about it. What if you form this vital relationship back with nature via a tree and what if the people in your life did the same thing, and then a whole movement of us joined you? Imagine how quickly connection would grow while separation shrunk. We would begin to reverse the movement of disconnect.

When a whole bunch of us reconnect with the intent, invocation, and focus of building a global human-tree forest, then we create a field of connected people and trees.

When we connect in this way, we are connecting differently from many other groups. We are, through intent and purpose, connecting ourselves and our trees into a movement with others and their trees which is a great global human and tree forest. We are creating a web of reconnected people in a field of people and trees.

Of course, trees are already in a connected field. Their roots join through the mycorrhizal networks, fungal root systems underground. We feel it when we walk in a forest, this living web; it is magical. We can also feel it with humans when we walk into a room where there is love, we can often feel this connection, or we can feel the fragmentation when there is no connection. It is us that is rerooting ourselves, joining this network with our own nervous system and roots that are also connected to earth. We are creating a forest of connected energy together, energetically creating a fabric. Imagine all those colourful threads, in which more possibility, more light, more innovation, and more freshness can happen from this connected place.

So let us start sewing, weaving, and threading, so that your connection is strong. Join us in the intent of this movement and practice to form a different energetic structure, or nest, that we all get to inhabit and create fresh futures from.

Chapter 4

Orientating to the Voyage
With the Earth, not
For the Earth

One day in a meditation I heard the beautiful, potent, and highly sensitised voice of *Papatūānuku*, Mother Earth, and it changed forever how I worked.

As we begin, let us start with Mother Earth. It is a voyage together; while you are finding your way, I am also finding your way, I am also finding

"Nothing for me without me" she whispered.

mine, yet none of this can be done strictly with intention or through thinking and planning. To begin with Mother Earth also means we begin with our bodies. They belong to the earth, they are earth. They are our most intimate relationship with nature. We will also be taking our bodies on this journey and learning to inhabit them as connected earth bodies. Without connection to earth, to our ground of being, we can struggle in relationships as it is our separate self, not our connected self, trying to be in relationship with another. Often, we are two disconnected and ungrounded or even disembodied selves trying to relate. It's hard!

Our bodies help us integrate our whole selves. Our connection helps us connect to the depth of our inner wisdom, a different stream than just our more conditioned mind stream. Two minds meeting are not the same as two embodied people meeting, where both are centred and grounded in who they are, truly meeting another also grounded in themselves. This is special, and in the mainstream is relegated to small moments rather than lived consistently! Embodiment requires that we are connected to our bodies: We can feel them, sense them, track energy through them, and we are connected to our emotional bodies and our mind. It is a big capacity to develop if we have lost it.

How amazing would it be if we all inhabited ourselves with that consciousness and orientation to life?

Without connection to earth, to our ground of being, we struggle in our relationships.

As we discover our earth body, and then our natural relatedness with earth, we can yield, relax into this great holding, allow ourselves to be held, and truly experience what being held feels like. We no longer need to hold ourselves so much or hold on to a perception of control. As we yield to being held, our felt sense opens up and our rigid bracing patterns can turn us to *embracing*. We can embrace ourselves in each moment with what we are experiencing and no longer brace against life and its overwhelms.

This is also a soft voyage, a process of gentling, of melting into the tender and delicate nature of our body system, the sublime and tender nature of our invisible but feelable fibres that extend out from us sensing always into the world. We have cut this off. We have ignored this. We have overridden our systems and we are unable to know when/if we are in danger anymore. We have sledge-hammered our system and we must find our way back to the magical sensitivity of our true being, an instrument of wonder and refinement. It is exquisite to feel yourself like this again!

Deep within, we are hardwired for, and we yearn to embrace, a love-making process with the natural world, just as we are meant to connect with our physical bodies. It's in the very fabric of who we are. It is a rhythm we can remember, catch, attune to, and flow with. The air we breathe, the wind on our face, the eating of food is all very sensual, if we but slow down and enter the experience. Imagine if all our felt and sensed actions and activities became a dance, a reciprocity movement of life—of us in the web of things, in the tapestry of life. If we can remember how to return to the wisdom and felt sense of our bodies, we can also remember our inborn connection to nature, and specifically, trees. There is so much in us that can come to life in this process of befriending a single tree. It can also help us re-rhythm, get out of rhythmic patterns that keep us separate. They are hand in hand, this connecting back to self and to nature.

It is a remembering of tree language. It is not lost; the trees have not lost it, we have.

Trees are portals into the natural world, into the deeper layers of the Earth, into patterning and into the light. They are communal, linked underground by large networks, always communicating with others, connecting and whispering to subconscious layers within us. We need to dare and bear slowing down; there is so much slowing needed. Trees breathe, sing, dance, and speak to us in a slower rhythm, but if we are living in an activated, up-regulated nervous system state, we miss these subtle communications.

And the whispering is important. Trees don't shout! We need to still, to find an inner space, a silence, in order to hear the whisper. So much busyness creates great activation and noise today. It is much harder to hear ourselves and the whisper of the trees, of nature reaching out to us. This process is to help discover the depth, the silence, the stillness in you, as you deepen your relationship with your tree.

There is much wisdom they have to share: Attune, listen, and come into intimacy.

Chapter 5
Capacity Building Together

This reroot route we are heading into is more like a spiral than a path. It holds the elements that are vital in this process of bringing ourselves back into the web of life. The processes develop a range of competencies that are part of being human yet have been forgotten. You will start to build these capacities within as you take this journey. These new abilities will re-*source* you, enabling you to inject them into your life. Just as all relationships deepen us, grow us, stretch us, call us into more of ourselves, so will this relationship.

Importantly, this process of befriending a tree is a healing one. I so honour the healing journey; it has delivered much to me in terms of being able to more fully live and express myself into the world. Many try to bypass this journey of internal healing; I don't recommend that.

Healing is a challenging journey and such a rewarding one. It is liberating to no longer be afraid of yourself and your interiority. Many of the processes have a healing orientation. Transmuting and transforming the past is a capacity and an orientation to life. How we work with the past—our own and our intergenerational past—can become a great adventure in our lives, or it can haunt and hurt us and others. When we befriend a tree and learn how to tune in, listen and learn from her, and feel deeper into ourselves and how we operate as a sensing being, we can develop a more stable base to relate more sensitively to others.

Developing a sense-feeling capacity is an amazing quality that is fundamental to this relationship; it is wordless. As we grow into it, we become more aware, more in tune with our deeper selves, our inner being. Everything arises in our perception. We begin to feel it and our relationship to it as it arises within. As we develop this, we start to experience the magic of life. We learn to truly experience the connectivity that is always going on across species and into nature, to feel into the connective tissue *already* there, and the beauty of that. This helps us turn on our ability to receive, to receive life, life's information, turning on your own wise council that sits within your heart. This is a powerful ability, quality, and serum, and it is worth the effort!

This capacity we are building is all about attunement, where we bring our feeling and our sensing together. I don't just think about myself or the tree or the space between or just look at my tree, I actually feel it, sense it, can sense-feel myself and my tree in me. As we develop our proficiency, we will also feel the tree sensing us! It takes a bit of time, but we will develop it as we go. For many of us, this natural ability that enables us to be in our true and very real connectedness has been hurt and shut down.

It is a daunting challenge to reclaim our natural ability to listen, feel, hear, and respond across the perceived barriers between us and other species on this living planet. The separating brutality of colonisation and other major collective traumas such as capitalism have done a fine job in making us think not only that white people are superior, but that humans are superior. There is so much to turn around and face and much to transform and reweave. We have done much damage to the planet and to indigenous people who knew how to be *kaitiaki*, guardians, and how to be in relationship with nature. We need to be able to untether something in us, so we can do this knitting of ourselves and our connectivity back into its natural state.

It is incredible to build this capacity and it helps us in relation to the natural world and the signals it is always sending through our system, to our system, and with our system.

Consider that we all have an "inner sea." Consider the body as representative of the planet. We have levels and layers, a biosphere not unlike that of Earth. Think of the makeup of the Earth and that we also have many of the same elements within the physical body and consider how the water content of both the human body and the planet are also similar.

As we deepen our listening and tuning into what is going on in our inner sea, words are helpful as navigational tools in developing this sense-feeling. You can return to *what am I noticing in my body?* Especially during the exercises when you wander too much into your mind. Here are some words to play with to describe what is happening to the energy flowing through and within your inner sea: tingling, fluttering, pulsing, thick, dense, shaky, numb, dizzy, watery, fiery, airy, strong, hot, pulsing, prickling, spacey, tight, pressured, contracted, wobbly, itchy, deadened, dulled, trembling, expanding, pounding, spacious, expanded. Maybe create your own list as you travel.

By tuning in more directly to your body you can start to feel how the systems within are always trying to harmonise. They are always responding and meeting what is happening in the universe! This rewiring out of separation to connection is a spiralling path; we spiral with processes of undoing the old, disorientating our conditioned way of seeing and being, then seeing and sewing in the new, connected ways.

As we develop on our relational journey, our exchange and communication of presence with our tree, we learn another capacity: we learn to replace and ground ourselves to be right where we are and where we live. Your tree is likely to not be far from you, so you will root deeper where you live.

We were all indigenous to this planet somewhere, so consider that our ancestors and ancestral rivers and connections are still available to us. While we are not all indigenous in our way of being and we may not be indigenous to the country in which we live, this does not mean that we cannot connect where we live; in fact, we must. *Papatūānuku*, Mother Earth, always wants us to connect. We can always pick up the mantle of guardianship wherever we live.

Indigenous people know how to do this; my ancestors knew this intimately, and we are recovering so much of this knowledge. Let us learn in this process to also listen to the stories and people who already know how to listen and relate to the land.

It is only in this connection to the web of life, and a felt sense of it, that we will come back together. So many relationships need to be restored, such as the relationship with indigenous people around the world who have these capacities for connection that we so need. Many in my culture, Māori, know much about this reconnection process. What indigenous people in your country still have this ancient intelligence? How can they help you re-enter your own holistic paradigm, an interconnected one, in the land where you live? Most indigenous cultures are based on relationship and connection. They will have specific intelligence to add on this path to global restoration. How can we honour this intelligence, learn from it, and reconnect and help restore the history of violence on these people and this vital intelligence?

To communicate with a tree, you must stop foregrounding all your usual ways of being. Put them into the background and bring your childlike innocence of learning and sensing and curiosity into the foreground. You must feel your helplessness, the place where you have no idea what you are doing, and then do it anyway, diving into that helplessness as a portal into the connection. If you can get there and stay there, it will open. These are also big capacities you can develop while we travel together: vulnerability, the gift of helplessness, of not knowing, and mostly the vital capacity of knowing how to intimately connect.

As you learn to connect, both within and without, you will also learn to repace yourself, create off ramps from the busy highways of life that keep you in sympathetic or dorsal states, or in a semi-state of aliveness. Repacing allows us to enter that natural current of life, the evolutionary flow. It helps us learn to settle, ground, and refind our earth body nature.

From this pace, place, and capacities, we then can regenerate, repower, experiment, create, and play. We generate from connected places, all bringing our own power and medicine back into our lives. We proliferate into the world all our magic from these connected, created centres in ourselves. We bring joy back into our lives and we get to express our creativity into the world.

Chapter 6

Contemplation and Creativity are Wise Guides for Us

We are continuing to explore the resources for your journey before we begin as they are necessary for the processes to come. These are two abilities you can build that will be generous and wise companions for you.

Contemplation is another key feature and capacity of this voyage. Contemplative life is such a beautiful way to live. It puts a river of depth into our life. It can turn a robotic life into a soulful life. It can help us find meaning and learning and richness in whatever shows up in our life. It, like tree whispering, is a gentle path. We do not hunt ourselves; we allow our contemplation to reveal to us what is ready to be revealed and no more. Small insights have transformative power similar to the art of inquiry; inquiry is not about knowing and is not really about finding out. It is about slowly uncovering. It is about asking the questions and walking with them until insights come. It requires patience. Contemplation is about dipping into the deeper rivers of yourself to see what is ready to surface in the service of your evolution and of course *then* our evolution. I call it "evoluting"!

Everything in this journey is about contemplating. It isn't about getting to an outcome or being a perfect tree companion or human. It is about rejoining the great web and flow of life with its rivers and currents. Secrets will be revealed when ready and they turn into crystal clarity as our guides. Like in any relationship, we spiral back into not knowing and into discovery, always spiralling up and down within ourselves and our relationships.

Our interiority, our internal landscape, will not unfold to us if we approach with forcing or judging; it opens to us with great gentleness and tenderness. Contemplation is not an academic process; it is a process of love. It is another creative art that is a great accompaniment into the mystery of life. What I love about it is that it is different from mindfulness in that it isn't about just noticing the mind but about participating with the mind, about engaging the mind and bringing it into service of the soul or heart.

Contemplation is a process of love. Many of the processes will use contemplation as a means of discovery and relationship making. You will learn this great and timeless art as you move through them.

All these capacities are qualities of being more than doing. People get caught up in doing. This work is not about the spirit of doing, it is about the spirit of reclaiming our natural capacities of being that we have lost in the busy trauma highways of constant doing.

Creativity is also vital in capturing the whispers, the ah-has, and the insights, creating and expressing your unfolding. There is an invitation to wildly unleash your creativity in this process.

This relationship with a tree requires a deep relationship with our own being. It will change us.

It matters. Creativity helps us go beyond the rationality that has been wired in at the expense of intuition and sense-feeling. It helps us work with the powerful sense of imagination that can take us into other ways of seeing and experiencing the world. Creativity is something we all have; it isn't about being able to draw well or do anything creative well, it is about finding our innate creative impulse and letting it unfold into something. Sensing into something and being able to feel another being is part of what we need to recover on this journey; it is natural to us.

You want to creatively capture this journey of ripening yourself and the connection with your tree, once you have found it, each time you visit it. There are layers to this capturing and expression: what you notice about yourself, what you notice about your tree, and what you notice about the growing relationship. You want to capture the whispers you hear so they can help you create your own myth that you pass on as embodied dreams to future generations. You will find the "Unfold your Myth Process" later in the book; however, the capturing each time you visit of what you notice will help you paint this myth and create this river of deeper knowledge.

You may have one whisper per visit really come to you from your tree. Just one. Like the dream catchers, you will learn to catch this whisper and weave it into your life. You can catch them, write them, and they become your living poem to guide your life, your own sacred text.

Creativity and expression also help embed learning in the trillions of cells in your body! Here are some suggestions for bringing contemplation and creativity together. You may well have your own practices and by all means just work with them or try some of these as well.

Below are gentle suggestions for you, not a list of instructions. They are to give you inspiration and ideas for your use. See what calls to you to start with, and later you may try others. There are also suggestions at the end of most of the processes.

Journalling

This is a wonderful art which helps you to uncover, discover, and unearth great precious gems within. To help capture this journey and embed these capacities, I invite you, and bossily would love to instruct you, to start a journal as you begin this process to record your "noticings" as a living experiment. Your process of the unfolding relationship will not be mine or someone else's, your relationship with your tree and "tree worlding" will not be the same as others, just like how no two human-to-human relationships are exactly the same. The journey of tree relating is a "rivering" journey, a flowing one, a dismantling one, an undoing one; one where you don't go in a straight line. It will take you places you cannot plan for, where you start to *river* with your tree in a flowing relatedness. Find ways to capture all this in your journalling, with not only words, but pictures, images, things you collect, anything you want. It can be a creative journal itself that goes outside the normal bounds of journal making. Let it capture and record the changes you notice: in you, for you, with you, around you, with your tree, and in the "betweenness" of you both.

Probably both your journal and your pencil (a good pencil is always better than a pen) are likely to be made of tree. Find ones that feel good to you. Always notice what is disorientating in each process. In tree communication, we head towards, harvest, and love the disorientations. There is good news: Our brain is rewiring. Celebrate and capture the disorientations.

You can time yourself with each visit to your tree and just free write for five or ten minutes, writing as a stream of consciousness, not editing. If motivated or soothed by music, you could put on a song and write for that amount of time. You could draw an outline of your tree on a piece of paper and write whatever comes within that shape. You can create a visual journal or add any drawings, doodling, or cut outs. You can paste things in the pages that you gather near your tree. It is a tree journal; what other ideas do you have for creating and connecting with your tree?

Poetry and Song Mapping

While connecting with your tree, you can also capture words or whispers, just a few each visit, that may not make sense and over time weave a poem or song for yourself. Just write words down that come to you. Brainstorm, or better still, heart-storm the words or insights that arise, without too much thought for sense making. These words can be the bricks and you can add mortar when you are farther along the journey. The world is full of too many disembodied words and a few connected words can be so potent. Then, when you have time, you may refine your words into a short poem or Haiku or a song.

There are many different forms of poetry; you may already have your favourites and use them. If not, and if poetry making calls to you, research poetry forms and use them as structure and bones, like the branches of a tree, for your leaves of words to hang from.

You can be as ordered, messy, or chaotic as you feel, and each time you visit you may feel differently. You can also find ancestral words from your deep belongings and weave them into your poems or songs. You can collect words from many visits and then write them all into one poem, not even worrying about the order, and let time fold in on itself. These are all just ideas for you to consider, experiment, and play with. These types of processes do help with becoming intimate with a tree, which is an experimental process, and this is why we are not trying to make it too serious as we capture our journey. The experimentation here itself helps build the capacity in us we need.

Prayers

Prayers do not have to be prescriptive. They can vary with the fluctuations of the heart. You can go to your tree or sit in nature and see what comes forth. Each time you visit, you can write a prayer. Capture your longing, your "honourings" (those things you honour), your gratitude in a prayer to the universe, to the natural flow of life. These can form your own prayer book.

Sashiko

This is the art of Japanese mending, where you make the wound or tear in the fabric visible and accentuate it with beautifully coloured thread and stitching. You could take this concept into your creative practice with your tree. Purchase a plain T-shirt and some embroidery thread, all different colours, some scissors and needles, and towards the end of each visit, express your felt sense of your experience by sewing some threads into your T-shirt, in whatever colours, images, or patterns feel good at the time. Imagine what the T-shirt might look like at the end of this journey. Or just use some fabric you have that you want to put later into your home to cover something, or to put on an altar you may have.

Drawing, Painting, Image Making

You can try sketch paper and pencils for connecting with your tree. Black paper can be especially revealing and fun! It makes a difference to me as a relatively new drawer.

Each time you draw your tree, it might look the same but as you see your sketches, no matter how rudimentary, they will reveal something of the journey of your tree and of your growing sensitivity to notice it and its trust in you to reveal itself in different layers.

You can do this symbolically as well as realistically or instinctively with colours and shapes.

Like capturing the whispers, each visit you could just capture one or two brush strokes and over the entire process of this book you create one picture, with each visit being one holon, a small microcosm of the macrocosm, a fully formed part of a much bigger picture you may not see until the end.

If you are a painter or a drawer, use these talents to help you enter the relationship with your tree; they really help.

Music Making

What beauty there is in making music with your tree whether you are a musician or not.

Try knocking two stones together to make a beat, a rhythm with them, under your tree. It is always different, and then you can add your voice to it, with a hum, toning, or singing, depending on what arises. Any instrument is wondrous with nature. Take it with you and see what comes to you to express your visit.

Sculpture Making

You can create land art if that calls to you. Look at the work of Andy Goldsworthy to see magnificent land art made from what is there. While at your tree, you can look around, see what sorts of gifts from nature get your attention, then make a wee sculpture out of fallen leaves, sand, or stones to represent your visit.

Movement Making

Using your body to express the relationship with yourself and your tree is also amazing practise. This can, like the other creative expressions, be quite diverse. It might be just taking a gesture, seeing what your body wants to do in the moment, then moving into another gesture. It can be free moving, tapping into the connective tissue between you and showing how that is by letting your body move to it. You can create a dance or a set of patterned movements that express your thanks or gratitude; it could be part of your arrival or leaving ritual. You could create your own *qigong* type flow of gestures. You can be spontaneous. You can also feel the different elements within you, air, water, earth, fire, ether, and give them expression.

There are so many possibilities; these are just a few suggestions to show you how diverse creative capture can be. These are the ones I draw from and will suggest as we go through the processes but please do what works for you to give a go, or perhaps there is something you are already doing that you can deepen. That is what is important. Try to ensure you always do something that creatively physicalises your visit through self-expression. It helps the rewiring.

Chapter 7
Taking Children on the Journey

For those who have children, this short chapter is to encourage you to take them along with you on the journey when it's possible. In some ways, children are closer to their connective selves than adults, depending on how safe they feel. Undertaking this voyage with children you are close to could be rewarding for you and empowering for them as they get to be the teacher and also get to grow the capacity in them before it is shut down by life in the mainstream paradigm which separates and over-mentalises. It can also help us bring out our inner child, which knows how to play.

Children are amazing at imagination and this process can give them plenty of opportunity to create worlds with their tree. Children who use their imagination and can enter made up worlds in safe environments are able to grow more of their brain, learn about their emotions and what interests them, how to adapt to situations, and how to connect to different realities. There are different stages of play with children; however, if you continue to let the child lead, you don't need to know all that because they will guide you in the way they want to play.

It is so good for you to enter their imagination and imaginary worlds as you explore your tree. Imagination can also open new opportunities for relationships and being with the sentient presence of another being, a tree. It can help us enter the world where this is not weird or strange but is, in fact, what can happen with ease and is the normal way of being. We are on our way to making it that.

Here are some pointers as you journey with your children:

- Many of the exercises and processes can be done with children. You just need to simplify them to the core offering and let them play with it and interpret it in their own way.

- Check what they need to feel safe; help them feel safe with you and with the environment. You can ask them if there is anything scary for them.

- Let their own inspiration lead them in choosing their tree, in how they want to interact each time. You can offer what you are doing, but don't make them do it too; see if they pick it up or have their own impulse.

- Get them their own preparation pack with their own creative materials.

- If they do have their own impulse, do yours, but do theirs also. Participate in their process (if they want you to). It's always good to ask, not assume.

- Always appreciate what they offer, whatever it is. It helps them deepen in their own way.

- Let them also participate in the creative expression later (drawing, dancing, chanting, etc.). Again, they may lead this.

- Enjoy their offerings and playfulness; it may be exactly what you need.

Chapter 8
Reminding Ourselves of Tree Magnificence

We are getting close to starting! But before we embark on finding your tree, let's remind ourselves and invoke the magnificence of tree beings.

This book is not about the science or understanding of the intelligence of trees, there are many amazing books about that (see the resource list at the end). You can even read some of them at the same time as you use this as your own experiential guide. The researchers are true pioneers, following their passion to bring the intelligence of the plant network into our understanding of the world. Please read their offerings to the world, the ones that call to you. They are true frontier folk.

Here are just a few tasty morsels to imbibe about the magnificence of trees before we start our journey.

The human eyes see a tree; the human body system knows with greater depth the gifts the trees bring, from pure experience. Trees are living beings, entities all in the process of treeing, and just like us they are verbs, not fixed objects.

Trees are now known to be communal, networked beings, talking to each other, helping feed each other, protecting each other, always communicating in their sacred *mahi*, the work they do in the natural system of things. Their underground networks of fungi transmit information for protection and allow them to share nutrients and resources such as carbon and water. These networks are like the neural networks of the brain.

The groundbreaking work of Suzanne Simard and others has opened up our very limited orthodox view of trees from individual things that had value for humans to beings of intelligence that care for each other, with even mother trees being able to recognise their offspring and provide for them.

And of course, they are indeed lungs for the world, producing what many species need, oxygen! Without them we and life itself would not exist. We cannot breathe without them.

They are networkers, collaborators. They seem way better at this than humans have yet learnt to be. Within the earth, they entwine and embrace each other and are interlaced with these amazing networks below allowing them to operate as one of the most functional families on Earth!

They do so much for us as humans. They absorb odours and pollution, gases such as nitrogen oxides, ammonia, sulfur dioxide, and ozone, and they filter particulates out of the air by trapping them on their leaves and bark.

You need them. We need them. They provide homes, food, medicines, and much more for so many species. They are an ecosystem in themselves: insects, bacteria, fungi, plants, mosses, birds, spiders, and the unseen ones all cohabit with trees. They keep the wilds alive.

Apart from these gifts they bring to us, they are not here to serve humans. They are magnificent beings operating at so many layers of consciousness. I believe they are contributing to the transmuting of trauma energy at this time. They are beings of light, as we are.

They also speak. They have wisdom; they heal; they calm; they provide nourishment for our bodies and souls. Their beauty, their attunement with season, their flowering gusto, their weird shapes and sizes and pure delight to behold opens the heart to life itself. Just because trees stay put, living and dying where they are born, does not mean they are not going somewhere special. As their roots go down and travel through networks underground to meet each other, they dance to a rhythm with each other and the wind that we don't always see. They reach out their breath to us and live through us. Just because they don't move with two legs, does not make them lesser beings.

Look up at a canopy and you can see how they often reach for the light and create a beautiful mosaic where each gets the light they need. These are some of my favourite photos to take, the canopy dancing in the wind creating different images with the space.

Even in their death, which without human intervention is mostly slow, they are a home and a nourishment to so many beings, the soil, and the future of the forests.

We must care for the future of the forests. It is outrageous what we have allowed and are still allowing. These are treasures, vital treasures, and we are losing them. We cannot. They are necessary on this warming planet and for species, including humans, to survive.

This book is not about what they do for us, it is about tenderly meeting, getting to understand, loving, and truly encountering their beingness. It is about connection, intimate and pure, in the hope and belief that this reconnection can reverse the movement of destruction.

Chapter 9
Please Meet My Own Tree Friends

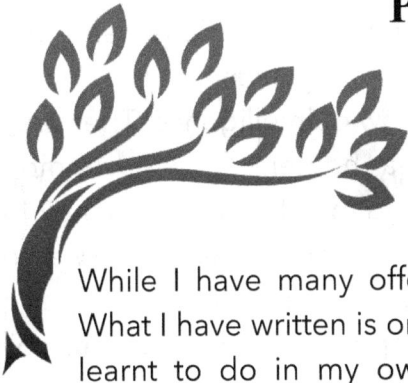

While I have many offerings, this is your journey. What I have written is only some of the things I have learnt to do in my own process of rewilding, of claiming my natural interbeing, of learning to relate across species, of immersing in tree worlding, of learning the subtleties in my own body to be able to feel into the world and practise being a walking tree—a rooted, connected self. It is a practice; we need in this new movement building of reconnection to practise our connected self every day until it becomes our new normal.

As we begin, let me introduce you to some of my tree friends, my TFFs (tree friends forever), just so you get a hint of some of the things you may discover along the way. We are going to focus this journey on you forming a relationship with one tree, and later in the book I will open it up for you to expand into other trees. If you choose too many at once, you can limit your experience of depth. Quantity and depth are uncomfortable lovers. I have many trees I live with where I live, and I realised I can be friendly and connected to all of them, yet I cannot know all of them with the depth I would like. Also, not all trees have equal energy or standing in the forest. Some are mother trees, some are connecting trees, some are medicine for the forest, and some are signals.

I love having different types of trees to relate to; they give such different energies. Some are *rākau rangatira*, the chiefs, the leaders. They are pivotal, often large, and their power is demonstrated by their magnificence. They hold a natural place in the law and flow of intelligence. They are a home for many, a signal, a holder. They have more responsibility. They are working for all of us, doing their bit to help these times. I have some of these trees in my web of relatedness. They are so wise. You can go to these types of trees with deep questions, for peace when in great turmoil, when you have uprooted yourself back into separation, or when truly lost and needing something to find you and remind you of who you are.

Another tree I relate to is a smaller flowering cherry tree. It has such soft fairy-like energy, is gentle and whimsical, and full of light. She offers blessings of playfulness, lightness, and whimsy. She reminds me not to be too serious, to refind my innocence. She is truly a haven for *patupaiarehe*, the fairy folk. Sometimes I hear them; sometimes I feel them. Sitting with her is sublimely sensitive.

Then there is the lemon myrtle. Oh my, how shall I describe her to you? She is a blessing, a giver; she is potent, humble, feminine, caring, and always offering her delicious leaves and flowers for my tea so generously and proudly. I also have a vine, an orange flower vine, with soft scented white flowers full of citrus smells. She is a remembering energy. She reminds me to look for the light in the dark, the good in the hard, the delight under the stone, the ancestors who are with me, and how I might be a good ancestor in the web and flow of life.

Then there is puriri tree, ancient, wise, and feminine. Soft and strong at the same time. It takes a long time to be in relationship with puriri. There are many layers of depth and medicine which I am still learning to fully relate with; it is as if I need to titrate her power within my own system. I love her.

Trees all have their own presence, personality, and traits. Just like our friends and our family.

As you go out to meet your tree, remain open-minded. There is not one type that you are going to meet; it doesn't have to be the big, grand, powerful ones. It really is whatever tree calls you, the one that is calling you right now.

All offer different windows into life and emit different signals and frequencies and offer a specific relatedness.

Chapter 10

Preparing You to Meet Your Tree

We are about to enter a powerful hidden force—a meeting of *mauri*, life force—yours and the tree that chooses you.

To start, you will need to consider both the prosaic and the profound, the inner and outer backpack needed for this journey. Just as on any journey of adventure, a certain amount of preparation and supply-gathering must happen. Allow yourself to stock your pack with whatever speaks to you.

The preparation is all in your own body system, gently, so gently trusting, opening, and sensing the web of life.

No two people will want to have the exact items; there is no definitive list.

At the practical end, get yourself a journal and pencils, maybe a waterproof mat to sit on, some gumboots, maybe a hat for the cold, your camera, and anything else you can think of. A water bottle is always good, and we will use it sometimes. It is good to build up some creative material like some coloured pencils and sketching paper of any kind that calls to you. You may prefer a musical instrument or painting materials. Whatever your creative practice is, find a way to include it.

In your inner pack you will need a willingness to walk in a holistic paradigm, one of interconnectivity, one where humans are back in the web of life, not outside it, not separate from it. Perhaps most important, come with your curiosity, your not knowing, and your willingness to be awkward, leaving behind the need to get it right. This isn't a journey to perfection; it is a stumbling, a wobbling, a daring, a delight of bringing the self back into wholeness and connectedness and the fluid listening of our water bodies. It is so important that you avoid judging yourself. Often on this journey, you will feel you are not getting anywhere, that you are a failure. It is because this is not about getting anywhere else other than in your own skin and body. Some days will also be better than others. It will also require a lot of suspension of judgement and prejudices about how outside-the-norm this might feel at times.

Trying to get somewhere in itself will take you farther away.

Finally, bring your patience along too. Rushing this journey won't help you. Trees don't like to be rushed. They have a different temporal appreciation; their lived experience of time is so different from most humans! Our own relationship with time is outdated anyway. Scientists keep telling us that time is not linear, and the mystics point to many dimensions of time. My own experience reveals a complexity of time that arrives in the now beyond what I can understand with my logic. What would it feel like to participate in a different perception of time? How might that change what you prioritise, experience, and create? What would this change for all of us?

Most importantly, don't work hard on this journey; instead, relax and yield, again and again.

The Art of Invoking

Let's also include in our readiness packs an invocation, which is very inviting (as opposed to setting an intention which often can be too goal orientated). The invocation comes from within and cites, requests, and calls forth that which is beyond our understanding, summoning help from energies unseen but very felt. This is the start of a sacred journey; it is worthy of some contemplation as to what you *want* to invoke. What are you wanting to invoke for yourself in this time? What would you love to happen for you? What are your deepest longings that this journey can help you honour? Poet John O'Donohue calls our longings "divine urgency," what is divinely urgent for you?

This may take some time, as often we are not used to seeing our longings as so sacred; take your time. Ponder these and then see if you can write what you want to invoke from that longing.

Longing

long-ing

be- long

not short.
Bring your long longing,
your sacred desires;
they are the language of soul.
Your own evolution calls you,
draws you gently through the
density of beginnings and into
the magnificence of magic.

Then think about us, all of us together on this movement, and us on this planet. Where might your longing collide with all of ours to create something alone, together? Think about *Papatūānuku* herself and all the creatures: How might your longing collide with theirs for a more harmonious future?

See if you can bring this into an invocation, your first sacred prayer on this journey.

Perhaps something like this:

I invoke the trees who are ready for this global forest threading of humankind to trees to call the souls and spirits of those ready to embark. I invoke the full support of the ancestors of the trees and humans for this "frontiering" journey. The nest is rich and nourishing, able to hold new futures for us all. I invoke the seeing of the web of life already perfectly in place and evolving, and I invoke the timeline that sees us all create from this connected web. Mauri ora.

What would you like to invoke for yourself? Create your own, even if you cannot feel it yet, just play and you can return to it later.

Word by word,
stone by stone,
leaf by leaf,
we return to talking trees,
a forest of upright
ancestors
speaking stories
with terrestrial tongues
holding up the sky.

—Dr. Karlo Mila
unpublished draft,
shared with permission

Now you have your invocation, your sacred doorway into your intentions. We are heading into the experiential part of this book where you will find your tree, get to know it, and fall in love with it. You can bring this along as you start your tree-visits to help you settle into why you are doing this and what you want from it.

Becoming Experiential: The Relationship Begins

The book now reveals a series of processes to help you find and relate to your tree. The first six you will want to do in order. Then there is a whole menu in different categories where you design your own process and unfold your relationship. Feel free to come and go, in and out of those as you feel called.

The first five processes give you a good foundation. Then you can play! Also, feel free to create your own by noting any ideas you have for yourself. As you go through this process you will find your creative juices start to flow, and your own process unfolds. Explore this! Even if something arises that you have never heard of before, invite it in! Nature speaks to us in different ways. Trust that.

You can return to any exercise many times over. Competence comes in the deepening. You may do a sequence of exercises that you love and repeat as often as you like. Try to at least give them all a go over time; they are together an alchemy that creates magic between you and you, you and your tree, and all that aids in your return into the felt sense of the living web of life.

This is both a guided journey and an emergent journey. Feel your unfolding self and where it wants to lead you, follow the trees, they know how to ripen.

Chapter 11
First Encounter: Letting Your Tree Find You

Here I will take you through a settling process first and then guide you through to meeting your tree. There are both actions and reflections. Read the whole chapter first and then come back to it and do the suggested activities. The activities themselves, the doing parts, are in italics.

Our mother knows where we reside;
she knows where you are.
Always.
We don't need to head out of
our skin and bones
to search and search or to follow someone else's
orders.
We head in towards our own fertile terrain

where we find the place that can hear the calls
of this tree wanting to find us,
this bird, this flower, this place.
This true you.

Meeting yourself first before meeting your tree is essential. Being centred and rooted in you, before you meet your tree will enable you to feel your tree calling. Before you leave your house to meet your tree, sit down and stop for at least five or ten minutes. Walking into your own "treeness" requires that you settle, connect, and breathe.

Before a person can successfully find their tree, it's essential that a connection with self is acknowledged—felt. This practice may take some time, but remember that the more you practise, the more available these small rituals will be to you; you will be able to slip into your own rooted self, your own walking treeness, with repetition; it's a beautiful practice. If you've never done anything like this before, please be patient with yourself. You may wonder if you are doing it *right* or if anyone might see you, or any number of other judgemental questions. Remember to bring along an open mind, curiosity, your personal invocation, and permission to attempt this and believe it is worth trying.

Guided Activity to Help You Find Your Sense of Your Own Treeness

Feel your body on the chair or floor; see if you can relax into whatever is supporting you. Let your outward breath guide you to release tension you are holding in and up, and trust the floor, the structure of the building, the earth, just a little more with each breath until you feel more present. Take some breaths and see if you can feel any energy flowing through your body, a streaming, your own internal sap rising. Feel the energy moving through your body, like two rivers, in both upward and downward movements. Feel the sea of sensations through your body; enjoy your aliveness. Allow yourself to soften, relax, and open a little— your mind, heart, energy body. Remind yourself of your invocation. You can say it aloud to let it resonate through you if that feels right. If it doesn't, no worries. Feel your personal invocation in your heart, and let it come from your heart. The mind won't and cannot make this journey on its own.

When you feel a little more presence and settling, start to connect deeper to your body by determining what delicious feels like in your body. How do you know when something is a true "yes" for you? Try not to overthink, just notice what happens in your body. Then feel what a "no" feels like. Go backward and forward between these so you get a sense of the difference for you.

You can use this each time before you visit to deepen its potency. The ReRoot course I have created to go with this book helps you do this with a guided audio (access this through A Call to Action at the back of the book); you can use this if you wish or do it on your own.

So many things get confused because we get these two things crossed. Remember, you don't need to try to get sensing practices right or perfect; you are learning. Keep relaxing, yielding, and coming back into curiosity when you start to feel you are trying too hard. Start the journey of sensing into your own body system. These sensations will deepen and develop over this journey, so no need to put pressure on yourself, just see whatever is there. We are beginning the opening of our energy system, the fields of ourselves, to become a tree listener.

Finally! You are Heading Out!

Grab your pack and start your journey. If you have a garden with trees, it may not be a long walk, as it is wonderful to befriend trees that live on the property you are already guardian of. Otherwise, decide which park you want to venture out into, preferably where you already feel there are trees that call to you, that you are already aware of or have noticed. Let go of finding a perfect tree (just like we let go of finding a perfect friend).

Some who have come on this journey already, were surprised at their tree. One man was called to a tree that was shabby and a bit sick, uncared for. He thought he might find something grander, but his relationship has helped restore that tree and restore something in him. Release expectation and judgement about your tree. I have had many varied experiences with trees finding me, and often, they've surprised me. Some of mine are small, but potent. Some are young, and we grow together.

Look for a sort of tugging within you, a beckoning, a natural stopping. One minute you are walking, and when you find yourself in front of a tree or plant, you pause. You feel something grounding you to the spot, and it feels as though you can't walk on.

Stop. Don't move on. This is your first tree friend. It is that simple. You may question this pause; you may even want to see if there is a better tree. This is normal. Trust the pausing of your body. Trusting the call of your tree.

You will discover on this journey that your body is always communicating with nature; it is nature connecting with itself, layers, assemblages, and confluences of rivers. We are many-layered beings and part of a universe, always in relationship with what is around us; so much is flowing through us in any given movement as this relating is happening. For now, just trust it and commit to the process with this tree.

It is good to take your phone so you can Google and check if this tree is happy with you standing on its roots. There are great apps that help you identify a tree (one I use is NatureID) and then a quick search will help you know if this tree is root-sensitive or not. We do want one you can get close to, so please check it out. Most trees don't mind the closeness if you are careful and respectful. If you choose one that doesn't like humans too close, you can always go back to it later and learn to be with it with more social distancing (something we now all know how to do!).

Once you have found your first tree, take some breaths. You are already breathing it in; it is already breathing you in. Put your hand on it and introduce yourself to it. You can whisper your name into its bark. Then pause, listen, give it time to be received. Next, you may want to tell it a little about you, not too much; it is a first encounter. What feels important to let it know? Tell it something real, like even how you feel introducing yourself to a tree. You can tell your tree that you feel awkward, excited, nervous, or any myriad of other feelings. You may recall again your invocation and tell it you are wanting to form a relationship with it. Let it know what you are up to and up for!

Then give it time to settle into the tree and the space and just listen. Open yourself a little to receive anything: any feeling, sudden ideas, anything.

Next, make yourself comfortable. Sit down facing the tree and let it introduce itself to you. Notice how this tree expresses itself in life.

Notice its movement, its colours, its leaves, and its smell. Notice in layers. There is so much noticing! Notice how you feel and notice what is happening inside of you; what feedback are you getting within your own body?

I get different feelings depending on the tree, because each one feels different, has a different vibration. Remember I introduced you to mine, one so fairy-like, light, enchanting, and another very strong, grounded, a mother tree, a queen, like an authority. Others feel playful. Others feel very strong like perhaps they have the capacity to be healers.

As with people, they all are a node in the universe with their own song to sing and bring into the world. Each is unique. See what comes to you and try not to discount your first sense. The mind is so good at bludgeoning our emerging sensing which is often what happened to us in our early life that shut this amazing quality down in the first place.

Sensing practice: Next, go through all your senses: smell, taste, hearing, feeling, seeing. Ask yourself what you notice with each of these senses as you tune into your tree. Then notice: What is your overall sense of it? What is your sense of its mauri, its life force? Notice if the tree feels happy or out of place. Sometimes this feels like it's in the imagination, but don't think too much about it. Does it need anything, something that you could help with? We will suggest this simple practice in other encounters, so it can deepen.

We are going to keep this simple for now, and we will deepen our sensory noticing as we go. Notice also *how* you are noticing. What aspect of you is turned on as you notice the tree? What does it feel like to notice? Can you relax your noticing, to be more sensing? Don't try too hard, it always blocks our sensing. This is important as we go to honour the capacity you are using and developing to sense. We are so used to valuing our mental process. This won't help you in tree relating. See if you can soften the noticing. Trees need soft noticing; they respond to soft tenderness.

Take some time and patch a few words together in any way that comes or make a sketch of the tree or part of it–a leaf even. It is telling you something about itself. Or make your first threads on your T-shirt. Or first lines of a prayer or song, whatever you feel like from the creative suggestions earlier.

Here is my small offering:

I feel the unseen tendrils
connecting me to you,
travelling on our breath.
I sense your breath rhythm–
your sap and my sap starting to move together
Two rivers in both of us.
Wairua

You can also just splash words across the page, randomly, wantonly, whatever comes with no thought for form, or if you are the artistic, creative type, maybe you do the same with a sketch, or with colour. Whatever your tree evokes can just come out of you in whatever way it wants to express itself. The more random the better. Some of that randomness may be from the tree.

Pause for a moment or two and notice again what arises in you as you notice your tree.

When you are ready to leave, consider how you want to leave, what feels respectful to you both. Don't just rudely walk away. Thank the tree for the meeting, say you want to meet again, and say your farewells in whatever way feels right to you. And leave with no admonitions for how you did, just appreciation for yourself for doing something that may have felt very strange.

Congratulations! You have your tree now to play with!

Chapter 12
Second Encounter: The Meeting of Essence Through Breath

For your next visit, start at home again, using the same practice to settle as in the first encounter. Or just sit for a while, breathe, and come into your body. When settled, then imagine your tree and see if it is calling you to visit again. It might be too early to feel its tug. See what happens as you imagine it and ask, "Shall I visit again?" They are usually always up for visitors. But don't wait more than a week.

Note that while it is good to settle yourself before you go out, sometimes that is not possible at home or work and might be better to do at your tree. They are perfect for helping us settle and ground.

We are going to do a beautiful greeting ritual for this second encounter. We are introducing and learning the art of ritual making, ones that work for you and your tree.

This time as you come close, pause a few metres away and just in your own words tell them you are there and back for relating. It is like stating your purpose and letting them also open to you. Then approach closer and put your forehead to it. Relax. Breathe the tree in slowly, a full deep breath in and then exhale into the tree. A sacred exchange of breath, a binding, a union. Do this for several breaths until you relax into it. Imagine you are exchanging your essence with the tree's essence. You are exchanging the breath of life directly, sharing this breath, the universal breath. Feel the wonder of that direct exchange. It is an exchange of life, of essence.

I am always amazed how this makes me feel in my body when I engage in this way with my trees; it is as if I do become part of them and they, a part of me. They all smell so differently, and in my tradition, we touch foreheads and noses and exchange breath in this way between people, it is called a *hongi*, a sacred practising of union making.

Stand back and do a gesture with your body of how it feels, how you feel about doing that together. Gestures are so good. You might just stand still and straight like a pipe, or with your arms flung up and open, like branches, or you might curl down and in, or curl into the ground. Just see what your body wants to do. Notice what the tree does. Sometimes I feel like I get a response, sometimes I imagine it. See what arrives for you. Enjoy whatever arises, whatever shape or shapes your body wants to take.

Then sit, notice, take time to come into the slower rhythm of your tree. This is such a gift in this fast and disconnected world. You are creating a connection, a thread, right now and giving to yourself and to the tree.

Given it is the second encounter, you can tell it more about you, and start to notice more about your tree. Go through all the senses again, as outlined with the first encounter in the sensing practice. What is new that you didn't notice last time? What has changed, even subtly, since last visit? There is always more to a friend than what we see on the first date.

You could tell it what you see and feel and notice. It often feels to me that trees have a similar function to mirror neurons, which operate to help reflect back to a person so they may deepen their learning and awareness of a part of themselves. In my experience, trees love being related to, noticed, admired, valued, and spoken to. Just as we need to be mirrored, see what happens when you mirror your tree back to itself. It helps form the connective tissue, the energetic threads that form between people, all beings, for relatedness. Also notice what you feel is most beautiful to you about the tree. Can you let this beauty touch you, meet you, arrive in your body? What touches you, what meets you? No pressure, just noticing. What do you sense that the tree finds the most beautiful about you? Can you feel anything coming back to you from the tree itself?

So much of this journey is one of opening the tender and delicate nature of your own nervous system, your own sensing nature, that can reach across time and space and species. We have just forgotten how because it got so bludgeoned and frightened. It is a slow, trusting opening that allows another in and that receives. Turning on our receiving department is not as easy as it sounds. So many layers have been switched off, and over such a long time that we need to learn to slowly turn them on again until we become a great divining rod. A pure, sensing instrument of life, of the natural flows of life, of the movement and river of our life. So much better to follow than the more conditioned mind. We can, for now, just imagine our heart opening and closing, something we can do ourselves when we need.

Right now, just practise opening your heart and see how that feels and then closing it, noticing what happens. Also see if you can open your heart on the inside to you, then notice what happens.

All these are practices to try and then notice what happens. In this way, we become our own inner scientist gathering experiential and phenomenological data about ourselves and the science of nature connection.

This will be a great practice of receiving for you. You will need to receive your tree which will help you with all your receiving in life. Take it slowly; don't force, don't rush. Our defences are intelligent and have been formed over many years of rejections and unmet needs, so let's not just violently burst them. Let's help them feel safe enough to slowly melt.

This tree is not going anywhere. It is still and consistent, open for relationship.

How can you creatively express yourself this time? Will you create a sculpture, offer a movement, a gesture, or perhaps some lines for your drawing or poem? Take time for your expression.

When it is time to leave, play with a leaving ritual for yourself. How do you wish to leave? What would sacred leaving feel like for you? How honouring can you be of yourself and your tree, and the land, the whenua it lives with? Feel into this. Create something that feels good for you, and you can always change and deepen it as you deepen.

Chapter 13

Third Encounter:
Honouring the Land

Now is time to honour the *whare*, the *kāinga*, the home of this tree, to let the broader ecosystem it is part of come into your being and awareness, to honour the soil, the land, Mother Earth, *Papatūānuku*, *Pachamama*, or whatever term you use to describe what holds the tree, what space it inhabits, and what its environment is like.

Feel when the time is ripe for your next encounter. We begin again with settling into ourselves. Try the same practice as in encounter one; you will build up a good muscle for settling. You do not need to wait to be in any particular mood. I encourage you

Our homes are alive, they are like wombs for us; they hold us; they encase us; they care for us.

to stay open to visiting your tree with your different moods, sometimes our undone states are the best ones to visit a tree.

Before you leave your home to go on your visit, take some time to connect to yourself and your home. What is your relationship like with your own home? Do you have one? Do you honour it and care for it and it you? What else holds you and feeds you?

Our bodies are sacred, walking sites and home for ourselves. These bodies are made of ancient matter, and many collaborating systems—digestive, circulatory, autonomic nervous system, endocrine, muscular, hormonal, lymphatic, skeletal, and more—all working together and communicating with the so-called outside world. All of these are operating with no conscious effort needed from you! See if you can slowly tune in to some of these systems. What is happening with your circulatory system right now? What is happening with your skeletal system? What is happening with your eyes, they are self-watering? Of course, many things can go wrong with how we treat our bodies, to these systems, but many things work and keep doing their best to work well. See if you can just focus on what is working right now. I love feeling into these so much, and the more I can tune in the more I feel the orchestra inside, always playing, harmonising, dancing. See what you can feel. Can you sense any harmony within yourself? We often focus on what is wrong. This invitation is to focus on what is working, where you can feel harmony within you. It is in itself a powerful practice.

Also spend time with the above contemplation to see what insights you receive. Remember in our contemplation chapter that contemplation is not about pressure because pressure will drive it away. It is a loving process, a curious one. You are connecting to your own wisdom, and it slowly opens more and more as you soften and inquire.

Now you are more prepared for a meeting of sacred sites, you and the tree and its *whenua* and community. A tree does not exist separately from the land, from the community around it. We will meet the tree's interbeing nature. It will help us understand and connect to the tree more deeply.

You may want to take something from home as an offering to the land and your tree. What feels right to you? It might be some incense, a stone, something honouring, something simple. Gather this object into your backpack and head to your tree.

As you come into its vicinity, stop farther away, and go slowly as you get close. Feel when you are entering the home of the tree, where its roots extend to, feeling into the land that holds it. Trees don't have walls to denote a home, but they do take up a home space. Take your shoes off and feel through your feet, acknowledging this land. Take the time to meet the land, to feel it, to notice it, to respect it.

Be open to what you might feel. Land can hold pain just as we can. Just see what you intuit. This journey will increase your sensitivity.

Let it all meet you—the land, the tree, and you are so intertwined. Over time, people have grown less in tune. We seldom feel the connection anymore, a sad loss. Today is just acknowledging, meeting, noticing, creating, and seeing what the broader space is.

Walk around three times one way, three times the other, and feel the place for your offering. Pay your respects to your tree in one of the ways we have already covered in the first two visits and tell it what you are doing. Place your offering wherever feels right; it is part of the connectivity. Sit a while and take in the totality of the tree and its home. Sense if it lets you in a little more. Honouring is always the way to be let in.

Nature always invites us into deeper contemplation. What is it inviting you into? How do you want to creatively express that? Whatever is present is welcome; sometimes in these inquiries, grief and sadness at what we *cannot* feel comes up. That is pure gold. Give that some expression because under it is the longing for something, for the connection.

Stay as long as you wish, noticing and going through the senses. Take your leave graciously and thank the land and the tree in your own way when you are done. Do it simply, with ease, and in your own authentic way in the moment.

Chapter 14
Fourth Encounter: Go Deeper into Your Noticing

For the next exercise, wait until you feel called to visit your tree. This one will help you go deeper, but only if you are excited to go. Waiting for and sensing good timing supports authenticity in your feelings and actions. This authenticity provides an experiential environment for your confidence in this process to build, familiarity to grow, and for a felt sense of meaningfulness to be cultivated by you and for you. Remember, this journey is not meant to be a burden. It isn't another chore; it is an opportunity for delight, a recovery. Friendships that become a chore are not in a healthy state, so don't let yourself fall into chore-energy state in yourself when engaging in this process.

In this visit, we are going to deepen the observation of your tree and what is going on with it. What do you notice? How is it living this life? You will deepen all the senses.

We are going to deepen the sensing practice in encounter one. Notice one sense at a time and connect to that part of yourself to see where your noticing goes. For example, where do your eyes want to roam? Where do your hands want to reach out to? Below are some prompts to help get you started.

It is always good to jot down ramblings or sketches, drawing what you see, feel, or sense. This can be done during your sensory observation or following just being attentive to the sense you are focused on. This is an attention-deepening exercise for you. You may well start thinking of more important things like dinner or the many things you have to do, but just like when you want to be more present with anything you are doing, attention matters, so gently bring yourself back and notice a few more things that arrive via your senses. Your attention matters for your tree relating.

Also know that you can return again and again to this exercise as you will notice different things in different seasons, weather, time of day, etc.

This task begins with simply noticing (giving your open attention to your tree and its environment with your five physical senses).

- *How does the tree look? Take your time to absorb all the visual delights: colours, texture, shape, light on the tree. Do the leaves come out of twigs or branches? Is there furriness of the leaves? What is the shape of the bark? Are there any flowers? What are* they like in all their splendour? Notice the configuration of leaves, and how they are arranged. Again, there is so much to notice, keep going into more and more layers. How old do you think it is?

- How does the tree smell? Take a minute and really smell the tree. Smell the bark, the leaves, the branches, and notice what you can about the subtleties. Let your nostrils explore as you inhale the tree. How does the soil smell around the tree? The smell of soil can remind us of our totality, and the returning to dust of our own bodies.

- How does the tree feel? Run your hands over it, gently. Notice how your hands feel as they run along the contours of your tree. Stroke its trunk, branches, and both sides of the leaves. Notice the difference. Can you enjoy the sensation of touching your tree? What happens inside your body, in your own sensations, as you touch your tree? Let yourself enjoy this fully and the sensuous essence of us stroking another part of nature.

- How does the tree sound? What sounds can you hear? Is there any wind? What sound is the wind making through your tree? What sounds are farther out, and farther out? What is the whole soundscape you are in, that your tree lives in? Can you hear any rhythm in all those sounds? Can you bring these together into one sound?

- How does the tree taste? Firstly, how do you imagine this tree might taste? How does it arrive in your mouth? What flavour do you get? See if you can feel the deliciousness of it. I don't recommend actually *tasting the tree unless you have thoroughly researched it and know it isn't poisonous in any way. If you have researched your tree and you know it is safe, you could give it a go. Just a small taste, to see how it lands in you, its flavour, and how it feels in your body as you taste it.*

- *What is your sense of its essence, its mauri, life force? Is it thriving, well, happy, vital, fully expressing itself? What do you sense of its beingness? How do you sense it likes its environment? What is it needing? Trees are networked beings; is it in a place that feels like it has belonging?*

After experiencing this task of attentive noticing, I encourage you to find a way of expressing what you have noticed or experienced and anything new that has come to your awareness. Draw, write a poem, a song, a chant from all of what you noticed. Keep trying new creative expressions; they really do help support the embedding of the relationship.

Chapter 15

Fifth Encounter: Practising Guardianship

Stepping into being a guardian is an important initiation for us humans. It means we bring our connection and active care for what other beings need in order to thrive. We don't own land in a true sense. We live with her, are a part of her, and we can practise our care and our love for her in connective and practical ways.

Have you ever had the feeling that people live on top of the land, without really connecting or caring for it? You can tell when you enter a house, a garden, a farm, if the people and the land and home have a relationship of love. There is reciprocity, a flow of vitality. We don't even own our bodies. We inhabit them. We are caretakers of these vessels; they belong to the earth.

How might you step over the threshold of relating to your tree to also being a guardian of your tree and the land it inhabits? Can you feel the doorway even as you read this? I believe this is vital for our response to our environmental crisis. We don't need to save or rescue nature—it has its own self-healing mechanism, its own deep source of wellness—but we can practise our love and caring along with our guardianship. We can help by ensuring that environmental influences like air, water, and ecosystems be as healthy as they can so that trees can heal themselves. As we know we have not done this well at all, globally. You can start very locally by seeing what is needed in the environment of your tree. Some things you can start changing, yet some are harder such as air quality. Let's focus here on what you can change.

I believe it is now part of all our purpose to practise this guardianship. Finding small ways to do this where we are, where we live and connect, is so vital. Most traditions have some history of this type of role. See if you can turn on your ancestral intelligence and recover some of the ways they would have practised guardianship. This could be such a beautiful reconnective journey for you with your deeper ancestry. What word did they use for this type of practice? See how that name lands in you, in your body. What if this became part of your purpose in life?

Next time you go to your tree, go with this invitation, and enter softly with your love, care, and deeper sensing. What does your tree and the land need? Sometimes these are practical. For example, in a park there may be chemicals sprayed that hurt nature, or there may be too much clearing, and there may not be enough trees. We can either advocate for healing this or we can change it ourselves. Sometimes, just the connection is needed. Sometimes there are way deeper things the land and tree are storing, and this needs specialists' attention. See what comes to you as you stop and ask and sense into what might be needed for some care. You can also research your type of tree and what it optimally needs and see if there is anything you can do. Practise care as you leave.

This initiation requires a deeper contemplation throughout the following week. It is good to build your contemplative abilities, so return to feeling and inquiring into what your tree optimally thrives on and needs to express its true magnificence in the world. Gather your reflections. The more we gather our reflections and the momentum, the river of these reflections, they inform each other and start to transform your perception through this cycling of reflective practice. It is another one of the life cycles we live in and one that lives in us.

See in your week how this continues to land in you and inform you, especially if you have found your own ancestral word for this. Feel into the layers of this and let this word and role move through you. Words, especially ancestral and indigenous words, have such a transmission to them. They open something in us, make something possible.

Remember to explore and find some way to express your journey with this role, how it lands in you, how it feels, what it evokes, what it calls forth in you. Maybe write your journey or draw or collage an image of what this role holds for you, and if you feel like it, please share with someone else in your life.

Also consider and research how you might show guardianship for the forests: who is planting/what is being planted; what initiatives of restoration are near you; how you

could support these. How might you join in planting efforts?
Planting future forests is something we all need to support.
Find a way to show your guardianship and contribute.

Chapter 16

Sixth Encounter: Sacred Names

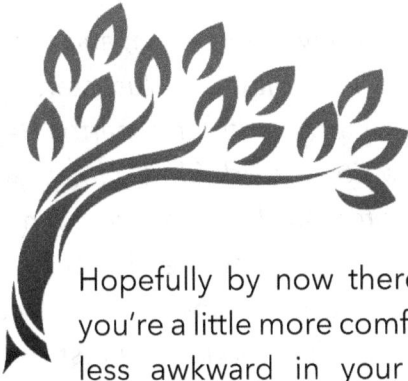

Hopefully by now there is a little more buoyancy, you're a little more comfortable with, or feeling a little less awkward in your budding relationship with nature and your tree. Allowing yourself to look forward to meeting your tree friend with more ease and delight, keep encouraging yourself to meet it as you feel today, just as you are. This is the benefit of having a tree friend; you never have to pretend or be anything or in any other state than what you are. Remember from earlier in our processes, the breath sharing? This is always a good way to open connection with a tree; it involves touch and breathing, and both will delight the tree and you.

Today is about progressing into another layer which will require getting to know your tree even more intimately. We will be continuing to build a warm familiarity by receiving your tree's name. It needs imagination, a playfulness. There is no pressure on this process; it may arrive or not. Tree-listening is a deep practice, a deep attunement, but we can start.

After greeting and settling and noticing again anything different today, we will go through a meditation process, then we will wander into dialogue.

Put your roots into the ground near your tree. Stand or sit and feel the bottom of your feet, with shoes off if possible. Feel where they touch the earth, feel that meeting. Imagine it as a sacred meeting and soften the barrier between. See if you can trust the grounded stability of the earth, and then trust just a little bit more, then a little bit more. Just start by entering into the possibility of trust with the earth, the possibility that you can drop a little, yield. Slowly imagine roots coming from out of your feet and moving down into the earth, down into the topsoil, through to the clay or next layer of soil, through underwater streams, down, kilometres down where they grow huge and wide and long and strong and beautiful. They entwine deep down in the earth with the other tree roots. Go down until you feel they hit some bedrock and they curl around it steady, connected, as earth to earth now, strong. Feel your own treeness. Imagine your roots and the roots of your tree entwined beneath the earth. You are meeting her nervous system; enjoy it and let your cells imbibe the feeling. Expand the trillions of your cells with it as you breathe in and release any tension as you breathe out. You can leave your roots down there, and then come back up to your body and into your heart and feel what the sun feels like on your body, your arms, your head. If it is out well and good, feel the sun; if not, just imagine the sun. Breathe in light, just as the trees do. Feel again your own treeness.

We often feed our cells stress and worry. Let's feed them the nourishment of the earth.

Reflection: How does being in this nourishing intention feel for you? What sensations arise inside you as you experience this meditation?

Feel if you are ready for this next conversation; if not, don't fret, you can do it another day, your tree is in no rush.

If ready, ask the tree if it is ready to reveal its name. Just see what comes to you and honour the situation by accepting what comes without judgement.

Tree language happens when words enter you, your mind or heart, without you forcing or making it happen through reasoned thought. Be prepared also that you may not get an answer, but it is polite to ask. You might get one; just see what comes into you. It may arrive as something that makes no sense to you.

These names are secret and sacred. There is no expectation to share them; instead, consider how you can care for this intimate information you have been given, this felt and sensed name the tree emits. This name is different from the process of having us humans name them based on western scientific perception of what this being we call a tree is. We have given scientific names to trees that help categorise them and understand them with one lens, but this process requires that we release the labels and allow for their essence to emerge. Their names often have to do with their *rongoā*, their medicine, their purpose. In many indigenous traditions, a name is given that holds the destiny and purpose of that person, for example, "holder of the purple flame."

If nothing comes it is okay; your tree is not ready yet. Name exchange is a soulful process. We give ours away so easily. Also be prepared, something may come to you that is *your* name or has to do with you and your purpose. Be curious. Write it down even if it seems so fantastical and makes no sense. These are the best.

You can also start to ask your tree anything that is present for you in the moment. Ask them a question of something you are struggling with in your life, then wait, pause, and listen for a response.

A response can come in layers. First, what would a tree say? What would *this* tree say, a tree with this much stillness and groundedness and wisdom, what would it say? Then what is arriving now, from your tree to you? What comes to you spontaneously, enters your mind or your heart?

Remember to follow up your visit with contemplation. What do you notice changing in you? Keep noticing subtle things or more profound changes, all are equally necessary. These changes can be in your body, in your thought patterns, in your feelings and in your mood or energy levels, or in your experience of responding to stress. Also keep practising your creative expression noting or drawing or sewing or dancing. Notice anything that comes in, whatever wild way and what and how it wants to express itself on the page.

As you leave, you can gently pull your roots back up. We will work with being able to put them down whenever you like later in the process.

Chapter 17
A Menu of Processes to Deepen and Sustain the Relationship

Now that you have established a rapport with your tree, it is your turn to decide what you want to bring to the relationship. It's always good for relationships when we are real and authentic about where we are at any moment. Why would our tree friending be different?

From here you can be more spontaneous and creative in your approach, grounded in your own authenticity of what you need and feel like in the moment. You have built the necessary foundations.

This process is divided into six parts, and each is fleshed out in a separate chapter:

1. Practising the art of tree whispering
2. Creating and playing
3. Taking your tree into your daily life

4. Healing and transmuting

5. Deepening into tree self

6. Going deeper

How to Navigate this Menu

Each section has a number of processes within them. It is important to see how you feel on any day and check in with what you need. You can also check in with your tree and see what is ready or ripe for emerging in the intersubjective space between the two of you.

When you know your state and what you feel like then choose from the menu for the most effective practice possible. This is a give-and-take relationship, just like all the others.

It is time to follow your own intuition now. You may do one process multiple times over many months, or you may hop from one section to the other with more pace. There may be one or two that deeply resonate with you, whereas another may feel quite foreign. It's very important to keep checking in with self. Just do you.

As a side note, reading all these processes just as you would a normal book could easily lead to overwhelm, so please take your time. Skip around, skim, or scan. There are no rules. Do what feels right. You can also just turn to one randomly, like you might pick a tarot card, and do that one. Play a little.

The processes in each section are in a flow. They do get more intimate as they go, so you can also do them in order, but this is up to you! Keep experimenting with your tree in a way that is kind and gentle, tender, and playful for you and your tree. And don't let these words get in the way of a good, intuitive, unfolding relationship. They are all invitations.

The deepening section may be best left for when you are more confident in your relationship to your new friend. Keep allowing the process to evolve, letting yourself slowly build more soil into the groundwork that enables your own roots to resew themselves which then allows for the unfolding of the relationship.

Please remember to focus on what you *can* feel, not what you *cannot*. Judgement on this journey will not help you. You will need to keep catching this because judgement will shut down your sensing; always come back to "what am I feeling?" (This can be a helpful practice in life generally!) Tell the judge to just disappear. Remember to not try too hard; your presence and playfulness does more than competence or proficiency in a subject.

Also, make up your own topics of conversation each time you connect. Try to connect at least once a week. Two to three times a week is great, even if only for a few minutes, and some of these you can do remotely by connecting with your intention and energy.

If you haven't the time to physically visit with your new friend, find a comfortable space to focus and try to invite your tree to connect with you from where you are as you visualise and allow the sense-feeling to ignite within. Initially, this may not seem possible to you but just allow yourself to be open to try and to explore this as a possibility. As with every relationship, the more time, space, and connection, the better it gets.

Most processes are designed to do with your tree. Some can be done away from your tree to help you deepen your own treeness and sensitivity and to make your next meeting just a little more exquisite. As with all relationships, you need some reflective time on the relationship and on your own being away from the relationship. Keep journalling or creating from what you may notice is changing in you. Perhaps you have begun listening with your body even when away from your tree. Maybe you recognise in moments you have the feeling of being *with* your tree, even when you are not. Learning to listen with our whole being is a capacity we as a modern society have devalued to our detriment and therefore lost as humans, but the good news is that we can grow it back.

What is Essential for All the Processes

The most fundamental thing to start with is to connect to yourself. Can you even fathom the fact that many of us go through life forgetting to ask ourselves "How am I?" or we answer ourselves in the same disconnected way we answer a stranger "Fine thanks, I'm fine," while ignoring the feelings and sensations we are living with in our bodies. I call this fundamental connection an "inner selfie."

Learn to check in with yourself several times a day. What is happening in your physical system, your nervous system, your skin, and your emotional field? What is the flavour and tone of your mind? What is happening in your availability for connectivity? What is the texture of your breath? What are the energy flows, the rivers, in your body feeling like? Does it feel like a beaver has dammed you up because you are worried, focused on, or ruminating about something in life keeping you from moving freely?

Feel out into the space a metre around you. What can you sense is happening there? Imagine opening that space up. The subtle layers of your body, around your body are always connecting, whether you are aware or not. What are you sensing out further in the space around you? Keep tuning in.

It may sound complicated—or even impossible—but it is a sensitivity to cultivate in your skills and mindfulness muscle and can be done in moments of coming into congruence with the layers of ourselves. It also takes practise. Let yourself practise as it helps create more coherence. We all talk *about* presence, but this is a practice of *becoming* present and synchronising to what is going on in any given moment. Letting everything be exactly how it is without trying to control and change. Even what you might be trying very hard to be rid of you can also include as part of your presence without forcing exclusion.

For example, consider grief. No one loves the complications that go with grief over loss. If you wake each day and say to self, "I am not going to feel grief today" and try and busy yourself, you are further disconnecting and creating a story, a façade, to be kept up. Over time, this establishes a miswiring, a faulty circuit.

On the other hand, what if you were to awaken and say to yourself, "Am I feeling grief today?" and you then wait for the answer. If it is a yes, what would be wrong with simply acknowledging without hiding from it or rejecting its presence? You may even look to see what can be learnt from the feeling. Oftentimes, allowing something to be, instead of forcing it away, allows for a timelier passing of more challenging feelings. If we welcome grief in all its many moods and without judging whether it is right or wrong, it may be that we can pass through the stages with more confidence and ease.

Lastly, keep curious about how you feel connecting to nature in this accepting and nonjudgemental way. It is important to notice what stirs in you in all the layers of your being—physical, mental, emotional, relational, spiritual—when you visit your tree and also how you are when you leave. This will show you and give you confidence in the magic of this relationship. This change is often quite subtle which is another reason for the importance of journalling. Consider how you feel prior to being with your tree, and then revisit afterwards. Does anything feel more spacious, metabolised, or harmonised to you? Do you find yourself thinking of it, even when you are away from it? Notice your dreams without resistance or discernment. Does your tree start to appear in your dreams? Sometimes, it takes a regular practice and reflecting through reading your words, that changes were, in fact, happening, but you were too close to see them while in them.

Refine Your Ritual of Arriving and Leaving

The sacred bookending of your journey is in greeting and meeting your tree. If we treat these comings and goings in communion with your tree as sacred, more opens up. It is important, but they can also become quite simple. The importance is in the intent and intimacy of your greeting. It may just be a touch and hello, an inward smile, mental or audible greetings in whatever way feels right.

Now is a time for you and your tree to refine together how you want to do this and what rituals you will create. Have fun asking your tree and listening for a response and then translating this creatively into designing your own process that feels right and can evolve. It may not always be the same which might be part of your process. Perhaps each visit you simply allow for organic communications based on what feels right. What's important is that your process honours the sacred nature of the coming togetherness of you both. This will deepen your development of being a sacred ritual maker, which you can apply to many areas of your life. How do you come and go from home, from others' homes, from other places you visit on this sacred Earth? How might you add a little more sacredness to that?

Chapter 18
Practising the Art of Tree Whispering

This section is to help you be able to listen and sense into your tree and the space in between you, with eyes and ears all over your body. There are some beautiful processes to experiment with. The purpose of offering these is to support you in opening up and feeling some guidance to do so while you are courageously embarking on this journey to receive the ancient language of trees.

Embodiment Adventures

Grab your body and bring it along on an adventure. To have a relationship with a tree requires you to also have a relationship with your body, *Your body knows how to connect. It is inextricably linked.*

and over time, your subtle body.

The practice below lays a foundation for the ones that follow.

Our body is a wondrous mystery, a sea of sensitivity and sensations always—and in all ways—responding to life. Learning to listen and track these rivers of energy through the body builds with practise.

Take time to get comfortable and do a slow inner selfie (the ability to present the layers of yourself to yourself— emotionally, physically, mentally, relationally) so you know how you are today. You will have a clearer snapshot of "This is me right now." Next, feel into your tree. Look at it and notice what changes in you. How does the tree feel in you? What do you notice in yourself as you relate? Connect to the essence of this new friend with your whole body. What does it feel like to you? You need to stay connected to yourself so you can connect to a tree, to receive it without force, as it comes to you.

This is a huge learning curve for many, to stay in the self and receive the tree inside. Sometimes, people get into "trying energy" which is not helpful. Relax. It is a subtle practice. Sometimes you may also feel your tree sensing into you. See how the tree changes the energy flow within you. Do you sense a new pattern emerge that was not there before? This is your tree communicating its "feltness" in this moment. Trees change with seasons, weather, and days, so this tree won't be the same each day just as you also shift each day, yet there is always something familiar.

Practise meeting your tree in this way with increasing depths of intimacy. You can feel into your water body—the inner sea we talked about earlier—and connect with the water, the sap of the tree. You can feel into your bones and from there feel into the bones, the branches, and twigs of your tree; you can feel into your own nervous system and the nervous system of the tree. You have so many systems, as does your tree. You can tune into any one of those and from there turn into the similar system in your tree.

It was a remarkable day for me when I could stand in a forest and exchange my goodness for its goodness. See if you can see this as an exchange of essence, of true nature, the specific nature of both of you exchanging. Even if you don't yet fully believe in your goodness, just find something, even one thing, good about you, and imagine that is what you exchange with the goodness of your tree.

> *There are so many "meetings" in life where no one meets. We are learning to meet ourselves more deeply to meet others more deeply.*

This is a must for capturing something, playfully, gleefully, fully expressing any doubts and failures. Enjoy the failures on this journey, starting right now. Consider at the end of the day asking yourself, what did I fail at today? What did I doubt?

By doing body sensing and feeling, we can see that it is how we learn to listen and hear our tree. How do trees speak? I receive them through my heart, mind, belly, and body sensations. It is like new ideas, or thoughts just drop in. It is a deep listening with my senses and my imagination. I still myself; I clear, attune, and open, just enjoying the moment of connection. If I have a question, or even if I don't, often something will arrive, whispery, gentle but clear.

Imagine those layers of subtle energy going out a metre around you like a circle. Feel that you open these, you are opening your field of receiving. This will help you be able to receive and sense your tree. The outside and inside worlds are always connected, we just have separated ourselves out in our minds. You will need to keep refining this practice. I know I will while I inhabit this body on this beautiful planet. You can use the vocabulary I provided earlier to help you become more refined in your body literacy.

Dialoguing

Now you can play with entering dialogue with your friend. A *korero*. A *korero* is a conversation, but it is a conversation with our whole being. Not two talking heads, two whole beings in deep relating. Keep this in mind as we go into this process as this process is more likely to work with this deep relating mindset.

The exercise requires questions and the above practice of listening. Imagination is always a good start! Imagination gets us into our right brain, which is so much better to tree whisper from.

You can dialogue with a tree about anything and everything. It's often even better than dialoguing with people. You can also tell it ANYTHING! Trees never betray confidence. They are excellent to process with. My tree friends have never shown they are sick of all my stories and laments, even if they do sometimes nudge me out of them! You can just let the words come, or you can prepare some questions. I highly value the art of good questions. Play with some artful questions; these you can use in many areas of your life. Always ensure you have some time to pause and listen for response.

You can go to any meeting with some questions and see what comes, but always do some attunement first. Here are some questions. Take time to write some of your own questions for your tree. You are asking your tree and then imagining the answers or seeing what arrives as answers to the questions. Imagination is always a good place to start. You will need to be patient and creative here to see what arrives. It is really good for helping us get out of our normal way of thinking. Give it a go, playfully.

- What have you seen in your lifetime?
- What do you see now?
- What are the patterns you see repeating?
- How do you feel about this time?
- What do you wish for all of us?
- What do you see needs to be given air, space, some expression, a scream perhaps?
- Is there anything that needs restoration?
- What do you see is vital for restoration?
- Is there anything we as humans need to do differently?
- What are the next steps for us as humans?
- What wants to evolve?
- Is there anything you want to say to me?
- What can you see of my life?
- What am I needing to pay attention to?

Or you may have a work problem, get the tree's perspective. It helps you access a different part of your own brain and creativity to approach any work problem.

Additionally, you can ask all the profound personal questions around your purpose, your loves, your place, your belonging, your creativity, anything to do regarding the arc of your life's movement. Ask the questions you don't want to ask out loud of anyone else; dare to ask the questions you don't yet want to ask yourself. Ask questions that may not even make sense to you. Ask questions about the questions you are asking. Are there deeper ones, more playful ones, more experimental and weird questions you could ask? Then stop, still, open, wait, wait like a tree, enjoy the waiting, and see what comes.

Deepening Your Own Tree's Story

Each tree has a story. Write the story of your tree. Research it. Find out about it. I haven't given this too early because our knowledge thirst to know stuff has gotten in the way of feeling and relating as kith and kin. But find out about your tree, what family it belongs to. How did it likely get here? Is it native to your land, or has it been introduced?

What is going on with your tree? Is it healthy and happy, or is it fighting disease? Is it thirsty, starved of light, or delighting where it is living? Is it lonely or has it friends? Is it enjoying being host to birdlife, insects, other beings?

What might you do for it? What might it need from you?

Also, what is its *rongoā*, its medicinal properties? What was it revered for, what does it like, what doesn't it like? What has it provided us? What can we be thankful for?

Time travel with your tree and feel into her life span and the difference between the timelines of you and your tree. Some trees have lived for such a long time. They span many of your lifetimes. Feel into this time span; what do you feel of the wisdom layers of your tree? What might it be like to travel back with them? Imagine you could and what you might have seen and experienced.

Write its story from the knowledge you gain, or even a short report, something factual.

Then put that aside and sit with your tree and ask it its story and pause, pause, pause, and then just start writing what comes to you as a narrative. What is this specific tree's story, what has it seen, what has it witnessed, what does it want, need, love, like, who are its friends? Just see what comes. This would be a beautiful poem to craft or a piece of prose to share.

Tree-directions

Notice your tree from all four directions, north, south, east, and west. Make a drawing of it, or take some photos of it, and notice how different it looks from the varying directions. Then stand in all the directions and feel the tree from that perspective. Make a gesture with your body to express how you feel the tree from that direction: its east face or its west face, its southern perspective or northernness. Notice how these directions also affect you. What might each one say to you, gift to you?

This seems simple yet is so freeing; let your body take the stance of each direction, see how your tree meets each direction. This is a good one for going creatively crazy with capturing.

Tree Rhythm

Visit your tree at varying times like sunrise, sunset, the evening. We know the seasons bring so much change, and so do these different times of the day. I love visiting mine in the evening, often a great stillness, watching their colour go as they become part of the night, pure black sculptures in the space. See what the relationship between your tree and the stars is.

Feel the energy the tree gives off in different times and seasons. I love the winter with my deciduous friends; it feels so vulnerable and generous of them to show me their naked bones. Of course, I also love the springing of the new lime green through the seemingly dead branches and twigs and the bursting of flowers so erotically. In autumn, I adore standing under the autumn tree and receiving all the blessings of the overripe leaves as they descend back to the earth, brushing my face on the way down. Have you ever had a leaf shower? Please try it, it is delicious. All times and seasons are worthy of our noticing, like what happens to the sap in them, their rhythm during the month, during the seasons. You come into a different rhythm in yourself with this noticing. We are not meant to be the same all the time; we "season" too. How does it feel to be a being seasoning? Your relationship with your tree can help you feel the answer to that.

I am at a loss for words, even though this is a word medium, to describe all the things you might see and feel, so I will leave it up to you. This is indeed one of the biggest adventures. Our rhythms are so interrupted by the busy trauma highways that dominate. This could give you some off ramps, some connection to your own primal rhythm and beat. I am sure you are getting by now that this befriending of a tree, this simple relationship, can "retree" you, renature you, rethread you, back into the natural family of things you always were. Notice, play, draw, dance, sew, chant, sing, and even rant—all is a wilding adventure, not a taming one. One to release the delight and surprise of living in such magic.

Getting Up Close and Personal

A tree is an ecosystem, just as you are. Now is the time to meet all the beings around and in this tree that call it home, their *kāinga*. It is worth buying a magnifying glass; get up close and personal. Take some paper and pencils and do some texture rubbings. Notice the colour of the bark and how it changes and what lives in it. Notice the back of the leaves; is the fingerprint of them all the same? What is different? Make up your own inquiries; it really is never ending. Take some time with this, maybe many visits, to see who you meet, who lives in and around this being. At first you may not see anything, but look into the bark, into the underside of leaves, always softly, always asking, always telling your friend what you are doing and receiving permission. You may dig a tiny portion of soil beneath it, careful not to be too disturbing. As you discover the ecosystem of this being, ponder yourself as an ecosystem too, a holon, a microcosm of the macrocosm.

What intrigues you? Is it the bugs, the small furry twig ends, the signs of flowers before they are there? What do you also notice is *not* there and yet you may sense? Some things are in the energy field of the tree and yet not fully manifest right now, just as they are with us.

Write what questions you have always wanted to ask about life, yourself, and this tree. Walk with them for a time;

don't hurry for the answers. Feel what walking with your tree and its wisdom is like for you.

Hearts Meeting and Beating

The heart plays a big role in relating to tree beings. We need to give it a little encouragement to open it. We have often had good reason to close it, and then we tend to let it close more often than it needs to. Our heart is so tender, delicate, and very sensitive. We have often had to shut it down because of our life path that has not nurtured it.

You can start this exercise away from your tree and then when you go on your next encounter, you have already practised.

Take some time to sit still without distractions, go inside slowly and softly, and begin to explore the terrain of your heart and the space in the middle of your chest. We are not exploring your heart organ, but the heart chakra. This includes the space on all sides of the heart. Feel into the space and imagine you have the key to help your heart gently open. First, open it on the inside, to yourself. Notice what it feels like as you open the space to you. Then open it on the outside and notice how that feels. Then close it. Play with that a little to see how it feels to gently open and close your heart space. No forcing anything, just invite and allow with more encouragement. Practise this in meetings, with your family, loved ones, or friends. Notice what your own setting usually is: Are you set for it to be open all the time or more closed? See what you notice when you play with both. Often, we need to close our heart to fold inwards and open it just to ourselves.

Next time you go to your tree, after your ritual of arriving and greeting, open your heart to your tree and see how that feels, then close it and notice that also. What are you more familiar with? Then sit with your heart open, wide open, and just invite the tree to touch your heart with her heart, to touch your being with her being. See if you can open to any vulnerability in you; just let it be here and with your tree. No need to protect it from your tree. A lot can happen in this exercise, so take it slow. The heart takes a while to trust that it can open, but often it does trust a tree more than a person, so give it a go. Trees don't mind if we practise on them. See if you can feel your beating heart and can you sense into the beating heart of the tree, its pulse? See if by chance you find a common beat or rhythm.

Also feel into the vulnerability of being a tree. Is the tree sharing her vulnerabilities with you? It is also vulnerable, in a different way, being a tree. We humans have not valued them as equal sentient beings with rights. We have not really honoured them. We have often imagined ourselves as superior. How might that feel?

Just see what arrives. What arrives in your body system, your emotions, your mind, your creativity?

Capture that somehow, it is precious.

Tree Presence

Sometimes, we need to go bathe in the presence of a tree and not do much else. Treat it as the friend you do not need to talk to or effort with. Please go. Just go and let the shimmering of the tree being gift you with its presence. Sit and receive it, like a shower of fresh energy, vitality, and light.

You may have a question, or a problem or just an exhaustion that you have reached the end of the road on coming up with a way forward.

You can start this practice with a bow to your tree, a surrender, and saying, "I don't know."

Then sit and receive with no expectation, just receive the blessing. In my experience, they don't hold back with a vulnerable and surrendered being in front of them.

I am frequently astounded at what blessings I receive and how much my state changes by just communing in silence and stillness in the aura of my tree.

Tree Speaking

I do this exercise a lot with groups and individuals to help them work with nature in a more biomimicry way. You can use it in the environment around your tree to help you notice things more and what they may have to say to you. *Look at and around your tree, and notice or gather:*

- *something beautiful*
- *something dying*
- *something ugly*
- *something exciting*
- *something mysterious*
- *something seedlike*

Then place them in a circle and feel into each one asking the questions of these objects:

- *Beautiful object. What is beautiful about you that you need to orientate to?*

- *Dying object. What is ready or needing to die in your life?*

- *Ugly. What do you find ugly in you that is hard to be with?*

- *Exciting. What seems exciting right now for you, that you are on the frontier of?*

- *Mysterious. What is your relationship with not knowing, with unlearning, with letting in pure mystery?*

- *Seedlike. What is growing in you that needs nurturing?*

Then ask your tree what it sees about these for you. What is the tree mirroring to you about your inner life? What needs to grow? What needs to dissolve?

Chapter 19
Tree Creating and Playing

This section is all about joy and enjoyment. We know relationships need work at times, and we need to keep connecting to the joy they bring. Try these out for increasing your joy quotient.

Tree Singing

Each of us has a song, a sound, our core sound, and it is healing for us. It vibrates through our body; it is part of our medicine bag. The tree also has a song. It is an amazing way to connect. I am always surprised at how the song of a tree comes through.

Sit with yourself first and start with humming, just humming. You will have a natural tone to your hum. You can close your ears with your fingers and close your eyes and hum and feel the vibration through your body and feel the sound of you. Let that sound go through all your cells. You can open your mouth after a time and see if any melody or anything comes through. Just see. It is medicine for you. Your voice is your own rongoā. *Take time to honour it and let your cells enjoy dancing to its vibration. Now feel into your tree, attune, sense, and just start humming again; see if it is different from your sound. You can let your mouth open wider and express the tree more through some toning. Notice what happens.*

This may take a few times. Don't pressure yourself or your tree. It is all about consent, not forcing; there is always a time. You can also stand and hum into your tree and notice what happens when you do that. You will often get a different hum than the one you started with. You can practise your own song each morning and night. It is such a good way to connect to your own healing rhythms held in your own sacred body.

Finding Your Song

A song offered this morning
to me, to others.
It is just that I am the one
awake
to listen.
Can you reach deep within
and find yours? Its
warp and weft, and colours
and taste and beat and heat.
Can you let it deliciously
unfurl in you like the
mamaku koru?
For that's what it takes—

a letting go, a trusting,
a silence, and then a
gentle release, that builds
and flows and dances
until it is you,
there is no you.
You are like the small
grey warbler, the tui.
Pure song.
You are home.
You are your offering to this world.

Create a Chant

This is a great activity to take your kids along with you; they are often better at approaching this playfully. Chanting is such an ancient practice in so many traditions. Consider your own as an invocation of your connection to your tree and to this earth. Keep it simple. I have one I do every morning that sews me back into the connected world at ever increasing depths. I have another I chant when I walk to remind me, I am the sea, the forest, the earth. Connective chants are powerful magic. They can be one line that you repeat. This is such a beautiful process of finding the rhythm, music, words, and a beat that feels good to you. Go and chant it to your tree; see how it feels. Does it ground and reconnect you?

Land Art or Mandala Making

Create your own land art near your tree as an expression of how you feel about it, how you are in relation to the tree. *Gather items that call to you and arrange them in a sculpture or mandala. Don't overthink, just start, and let yourself unfold into your sculpture. You can give yourself a time limit (start with twenty minutes). If you are stuck, it really helps you just get into it.* Then ask yourself some inquiry questions:

- *How do I feel about my sculpture?*
- *How does it make me feel?*
- *What does it say to me?*
- *What surprises me?*
- *What interrupts my normal way of seeing or being?*
- *If I could make one change what would that be? Go ahead and make that change and then see what shifts. How does that feel? Imagine that it has already shifted something in your world.*
- *What other questions do I have for myself?*
- *What questions am I not ready to ask yet? What are the questions I may not want to ask?*

Writing Your Own Prayer

You may want to write a prayer with your tree.

Sit with your tree and let your longing be there. Feel what the tree may long for.

Our longing shows us something about our soul.

I love working with the following headings:

- May I remember…
- May I receive…
- May I be blessed by…
- May I be a blessing…
- May I keep the fire alive…
- May I give full expression to…

- May I connect to…
- May I understand…
- May I enrich…
- May I surrender…
- May I embody…
- May I be of service into the world…

You can brainstorm words for each statement and then you can play with mixing them up with the headings and make up your own lines. You don't have to use all these. They are just prompts. Share your prayer with your tree. A prayer for yourself is so enriching.

You can also imagine what your tree's prayer is for its life. This is also enriching. You can use the same prompts.

Mythmaking with Your Tree

There are many myths about trees. Most cultures have them. Research some of them. Learn about how some see trees as symbolic beings that inhabit many realms, from the underworld deep into the earth, the earth realm on the Earth, and how they extend into the sky realms, their branches reaching to the light. They are seen as alchemists, always looking to turn metal into gold. These trees turn light into food and oxygen. The trunk is a pillar between *Papatūānuku* and *Ranginui*.

Mythmaking is another sacred activity; it reaches deeper than story. It reaches into the rivers of our being and brings forward the potent truths that were whispered from one generation to the next. Remember, re-member. I told you I was a braided river, and DNA testing shows us we all are, with pieces of Africa, our first mother, and pieces of the journey our ancestors all made from there. There are rivers inside you. There are whispers inside you, wanting to be heard and brought back into being along with potent truths from all the rivers and ancestors.

Your tree has its own ancestors, its own rivers. These have now collided together in this relationship.

Sit with your tree. Invite your own myth to flow from you.

Start with your tree. What is its mythology, what does its ancestors say through it, what whispers does it hear? You can do this both imaginatively but also research more about your tree, its origins, where it came from, who its companions were, what part of this living planet it likes the best, or what its ancestors might have seen. Who are its relations? Such rich fodder for mythmaking.

What myth is it unfolding in you? Mythmaking takes some time. They are rich stories that allow you to reach back into your own ancestral lines and see what words and wisdom want to come through to you and then consider what you want to pass on. Myths are truths worthy of being passed on, *needing* to be passed on. What is travelling through you that needs to be passed on? Have a go at myth making. *You can start by seeing your life as a scenario.*

- *What myth has been unfolding in you since the day you were born?*

- *What are you here to learn in your life? You can research the core myths in your own traditions.*

- *What has been your hero or heroine journey so far?*

- *How does it carry forward your ancestral stories? Our hero or heroine journeys are often guided by the learning we have done in this life through the journeys we have had to make.*

- *If you chose this life to learn, what life experiences are you learning through? Is it through loss and grief? Is it through power and distortion of power? Is it through trusting love when love can be so dangerous?*

- *How do you want your life, your myth, to change patterns that need changing and unfold in a more creative, full expression of you and your ancestral lines?*

- *What might you be here to transform for your ancestral lines?*

- *What is your medicine to bring into this world?*

- *What alchemy are you here to do or to transform what hardships into light?*

It is never a job. This is deeply your essence and its part in the nature of things.

Then I like to imagine and hear the whispers of the myth of us together, me and my trees, you and yours. This is so fun to create a myth from the beginning of this weaving that you have started and will pass along to many future generations, a gift of connection, rerooting. You might like to call it something like "The Great ReRoot that Changed History." Go for something grand; pour all your hopes and dreams for you and us and the planet into this myth. Pour your tree's wishes for this planet and her home. Let yourself take as long as you need. It might take months, this pouring of you and your tree into a myth, to pass on. You are restarting, rebooting; this is your contribution. When you have written it, make sure you sit with your tree and embody it, let the dream of it stream through your body. Myths are rivers and you have just created one. Feel it, let it go into every cell.

Imagine others writing theirs as you write yours, a collective myth making.

> But don't be satisfied with stories,
> how things have gone with others.
> Unfold your own myth,
> without complicated explanation,
> so everyone will understand
> the passage,
> We have opened you.
> —Rumi

Looking At, In, and With the Web of Life

The web of life feels like a current to me, a flow, an unfolding pattern. Webs are beautiful and of course they are also traps for prey. In this visit I want you to look closely around your tree and find a web. I am sure there will be one there somewhere, spiders love trees. If it is not the season in your part of the world to spot one, leave this for when it is. *Find a web in your tree, or around it. Notice all the details about it; see if you can write down twenty-eight observations about your web. Then create four columns in your journal: webs look, webs feel, webs create, my web is... Then put some of the words from your observation under each one. Create lines, putting words together from your observations, perhaps where you may not intuitively place them. Create a poem from these lines.*

Also, you can draw the web you see. I love drawing them with white coloured pencil on black paper. Try drawing your own web. You are always in the middle of your web of life. What does your web look and feel like? Look at all the relationships in your web, how clean and nourishing they are or how disturbed or disrupted. This is a profound drawing to take time with and then ask yourself some questions about. Inquire into what feels good to you and what doesn't and what you might want to shift or repair or let go of in your web.

Hanging Out

Don't forget that while I have all these suggestions, keep also just hanging out and having fun. Be spontaneous and free and enjoy every moment of it. Enjoy just being together and see what arises, just as it is with a friend; simply be together. Don't let all these suggestions get in the way of hanging out. What we have been building is a different way of hanging out with ourselves so we can hang out with our tree in a connected way.

Chapter 20
Bringing Your Tree into Your Daily Life

Like any relationship, we can bring what we learn from it into the rest of our life. We can bring our enhancing of our reconnection muscle into many areas of our life that might need it.

Six by One

Six times a day, can you pause for one minute and connect to your tree? Whatever you are doing, just pause and connect to your tree and imagine you are there breathing with it, yielding into it.

You can do this in meetings with your eyes open, or in front of your computer, anywhere.

This act of pausing will open up space, joy, and grounding in your life. We often wait for the perfect time to pause, like when something is complete, or before moving to another task, but it's equally good to pause in the middle of the thing that feels so urgent. This pause can bring life back into a contracted, pressured place. Give it a go.

Being Your Tree

Building on the above, you can also practise in those pauses being your tree, or being another tree, or just being your tree self. *Imagine roots out of your feet into the ground and your upper body reaching to the light.* Being your tree self can help you be joy-making and light-making in the world, rather than looking for joy. You can return to being a tree self as many moments in a day you want or need.

Tree Travelling

You can take your tree to a meeting, into a board room, into anything you need some grounding and support for. It is a resource in your daily life for you. Imagine you are resting back into it; it is there for you and for your highest possibility. As I said, there are so many meetings and yet often no one meets. See if you can bring your tree, silently, into the room; notice what happens in you and to the quality of the meeting itself. This is such a profound experiment, and you don't have to tell anyone.

Wouldn't it be great if everyone around a board table had their tree behind them whispering with their networked intelligence the next way to flow, the best way to river towards an evolutionary pathway? This is what it takes to step into a new paradigm and start to dismantle the one that has not served a connected world. You can also ask yourself in meetings, what would the tree feel or think about this, and see what comes. I have noticed that when people do this or talk about trees and connecting with them, their voice generally drops, they slow their pace which are all good things for breaking the busy with some deeper words of wisdom. Give it a go.

Meditate with Your Tree

Our tree can help us meditate by aiding us to settle into meditation. I have often spontaneously become a tree in meditation where I am very earthed into the ground and extending way up into the sky. It helps get me out of trying or "efforting" and back into my own tree self and grounded, not having a problem with anything that arises. It is a ballast, and it helps us find our ballast within us, a stillness and strength for which to approach the many arisings that often destabilise. Notice what type of tree you become. It doesn't have to be a certain one; it might be a mix of many different trees.

Orientate to Beauty

Think of your tree when you are not with it. Think of its beauty and feel how that beauty feels in you. Let it help you connect to your own beauty. We so easily orientate to the problem that exists within this moment; let it help you orientate to the beauty of this moment, in you, out of you. It can help be a great reorientation in you, a reframing of yourself in the world. The human ego loves to make everything a problem; this can help break out of that incessant problem-making and into flow-making.

Connecting with Nature Anytime

You don't have to be *in* nature to connect with nature. You *are* nature, and it is always around you. There are always the elements—air, water, earth, fire—arising within you. We are made of elements. It is a wondrous thing to feel into our own inner ecology, our own geography and landscape, a whole natural world within us. It is lovely to learn to relate to yourself in this way with sacredness and awe. We are a universe, and inside we are full of mountains, rivers, valleys, forests. I love to roam inside with curiosity, into the universe of me, the blackness, and stars of my mind, like a clear night sky. Can you enter yourself in this way—with awe, with amazement and all the rhythms of all the systems, and the space, and the stillness—and the magic that each part holds? I often think of different parts of me as being their own animal, their own being. Like hands, think of them as their own beings. Have a look at yours. What magic they are, what joy, how accomplished they are. Have fun exploring yourself as a whole array of nature beings, ecologies, landscapes, soundscapes, rhythmscapes, music, dances, delights, and mysteries.

Chapter 21
Healing and Transmuting

This section is for when you are not feeling great or feeling overwhelmed and disconnected, maybe even in a trauma vortex. They are so painful to bare. These processes are slow and gentle and simple. It will explore the healing nature of the relationship with trees. These are good to do when you are not feeling up for relating to anyone. This is such a good time for tree relating. See which ones call to you.

Letting Nature Cleanse Us

This is all about letting nature cleanse us by returning to our places of power. No effort required.

I have experienced gentle healing and clearing from my tree friends. It has been a beautiful practice for me to sit under my trees and ask for their blessing, for a clearing, for

Hoki atu ki tōu maunga kia purea ai e koe ki ngā hau o Tāwhirimātea

Return to your mountains, to be cleansed by the winds. (Tūhoe saying)

healing, and then sitting and receiving the energies that meet me. Try it. It gets stronger with practise, not because it actually strengthens, but because you are more open to the subtleties—you *feel* it more; you receive it more. Different types of energy come from different trees. Trees transmit and emanate healing frequencies. Open your receiving department. Open those subtle layers and all the protections we have, to receive with gratitude.

Then in the spirit of reciprocity, send healing toward your tree. We all live in toxic food systems including air and water pollution. Your tree body will feel this just as our bodies do. What would it be like to extend healing intention from your heart to your tree?

Open your heart, intend to again send your essential medicine and anything the tree needs right now from you. Reach out and touch your tree. Imagine that exactly what the tree needs and is asking for comes from your heart through your arms and out of your hands to your tree. Notice, feel, breathe, love.

There is a great book in the resources section, *Partnering with Nature*, which has developed a whole series of healing mantras to use with a tree. Check them out and practice what they have experimented with over many years.

Experiencing and Exchanging Medicine

Every tree has its own medicine, its own energy, that it is here to vibrate out and send into the whole. As humans we have bottled this, imitated it, extracted it, and done all sorts of things to capture it. We don't need to. We can just attune with it and imbibe it without harming the tree at all.

This requires patience and the relationship we are unfolding here.

I introduce this now because you will have a deeper relationship, which means your attunement to your tree's gifts and medicine will be less from that extractive place and more from your relatedness and curiosity. This matters. From now on, you can do this exercise in every process.

Feel into you and get a sense of what you actually feel like. That is your sense of you. What is your sense of your own medicine in this world? You hold a medicine also. Then have a sense of your sacred medicine extending, filling your being, even if you don't know what it is. The essence of you fills every cell and emanates out. Imagine this emanation as fibres or as capillaries that extend from your body and towards your tree. Imagine this sacred energy calls forth the sacred energy of your tree friend. Your tree is always emanating its medicine. Imagine this all happens a metre from your being, and a metre out from the tree where you meet in the between, the space between, and exchange goodness and medicine. Imagine every breath in is the tree breathing out and every breath out, the tree breathes you and your medicine in. This is such a beautiful breathing exchange to do for as long as you want; it will deepen beyond your wildest dreams if you keep this up for some time. Start slow and small and with every process see if you can at least do five minutes of this, and at times see if you can deepen to an hour. Feel yourself as you finish, always thanking yourself and the tree for the exchange, and notice how your body feels. Give some creative expression to this.

Co-treelating

Coregulation is becoming more understood in how vital it is for all of us, yet many of us didn't have it growing up. You can learn to coregulate with a tree; they are excellent at it. *If you can, sit with your spine against its trunk, feel the support. Soften, soften more, relax, and let your body trust the support of the tree. Yield. What does support feel like to you? Notice the body sensations, the images, any emotion. Breathe the feeling of support into every cell. Let your body relax and soften more and more into the support of the tree, into feeling supported. What does support feel like for you? How do you accept support that you know isn't going to go away? We have often not had the support we need so it may take a while to embody this feeling. Practise this often and your whole nervous system will start to unwind and reset at a more relaxed level. Let yourself feel it and enjoy it. Rest in it. Keep trusting your tree with your weight more and more with each breath. Through your spine, see if you can feel the energy of the tree. See if you can feel or imagine that energy as love. See it as life-loving energy, moving up the spine of the tree, moving up your spine. Two spines meeting.*

Coming Apart

Nature is so soothing when we are coming apart. It took me a long time to not panic when things inside were coming apart. It took great practise to accept and honour that this undoing was also sacred and important.

There is so much that needs to dissolve in our world which means it needs to dissolve in us, in the way we world ourselves, in our inner world. This is always a painful process, emotionally and physically, as it is old structures within us melting, and often they have held us up when nothing else was there to hold us.

Learning the art of coming apart is a work in progress. I think I have reached some proficiency and then I am forced into humility again by the greater intensity of the next dissolving process. They are disorientating, wobbling, uncertain, painful, intense. These times are calling us to be with this coming apart, as so much needs to change.

My trees help me in these times. As I sit with them, they represent the part of me that isn't coming apart, that is the ground of being, my true nature, the *maunga*, the mountain of being that always is. What is coming apart is the self that formed around that as a series of painful experiences and protections. It is really an imitation of our true self.

The trees remind me of this, helping me calm and settle. I contact, with their help, this whole place in me again to contact that place in them. A surrendering can happen, and I come back into some acceptance of the impermanence of things, the coming, the going, and what stays.

This visit is for when you are in this place.

Again, sit with your spine against the trunk of the tree if you can. Feel the ground beneath you, take some breaths focusing on the outward breath, making the outward breath longer as you exhale. Let your body keep dropping into the earth, trusting it a little more each time to hold you up.

We do so much holding and bracing of ourselves. We are meant to be an *embrace*, not a brace. We can learn to be held.

Letting this bracing pattern relax is often a lifetime of practising slowly and lovingly, because it was lack of love that caused it, so forcing is not going to work.

Feel your spine against the spine of the tree. On the exhale, relax back into it more and more. Let your nervous system find its connection to earth and tree and let yourself be held in these arms, from beneath and behind. You can sit and do this letting go, surrendering, resting, relaxing, releasing, trusting, and letting the bracing come apart for as long as you want. It is an unwinding. See if you can focus on allowing the chronic bracing most of us have, to trust the tree enough to soften. Soften, soften, and soften some more. Under this bracing pattern is often the pressure pipe we have put on ourselves. You may encounter this. I dislike this feeling so much; it is hard to be with for me. Feel your arms and legs and imagine that pressure-pipe energy can come out those channels and not get stuck in your heads or bodies. Imagine the tree trunk takes some of it for you and puts it down its roots and into Mother Earth. Share it with the tree and through your feet and into the earth. You can have a bigger body to process with. It has felt like it has saved my life many times.

It is such a good practice to incorporate into any visit.

See how you feel and take your leave with your thanks whenever you want. Maybe make a gesture as you leave. It is good in this one not to have too many words.

Grief and Trees

Trees are good at grief. I have had much grief and loss in my life. They seem especially good at it, soothing, comforting, offering a timeless perspective that is bigger than these bodies we inhabit. They are rooted in the ground and in the timeless. They have seen their own fair share of loss.

Loss and grief can isolate us, make us separate into ourselves, alone and desperate. You may or may not be in grief, or you may also have unprocessed old grief, as most of us do.

Make this visit the softest and most tender that you can. We need to meet ourselves with such love and tenderness in this place. Soft, so soft.

After greeting your tree, just sit, and get comfortable with your spine against its trunk or close to it, touching skin to bark. Then tell her that you come to her in grief, in sacred grief. The amount we grieve is so linked to the amount we loved. You come with love when you come with grief. Feel the support of the tree on your spine, feel the holding. Feel the substance of the tree with its groundedness. See if you can find that feeling in your own body.

From this feeling of the substance of the tree and the support you feel, allow what grief there is right in the moment, and touch into it with as much love and tenderness for yourself as you can muster. Like the beautiful infinity pattern, see if you can go back to feeling the substance of the tree with its support and back into touching the grief, without being immersed in it, not meddling with it, just touching it. You can try synchronising your breath with this dance and see what rhythm feels best for you. You can do this pattern as often as you wish and notice what happens in you as you do it. Again, you can share it with the tree in energy or with words. Just tell it of your grief.

Then imagine all the grief that this tree may have seen, witnessed, felt. Her waters may hold some of the grief of the world. Acknowledge your grief is part of an ocean of grief that we are all in; you are not alone in it. Imagine you breathe out with your tree for all this grief also. Never alone.

When finished, just sit a while, then maybe write a poem or letter to the person or situation you are grieving about expressing all your love and hurt.

Thank your tree for her support as you leave in whatever way you are taking your leave.

Your Inner Child and Your Tree

We have so much stored hurt from our childhood that is still in our bodies, waiting for us to be able to feel and experience them in a supported way so they can move through us and create more space and vitality for our purpose to flourish.

Imagine yourself as a young child. Let them sit beside you with the tree. What relationship would they have loved to have with your tree? What did they need to have support for? Imagine that they and you can lean on your tree to be supported, held, loved, resourced. Feel the support in your own system. Imagine a three-way conversation. How would you have loved this to be? Let the inner child guide the conversation saying what they needed, would have loved, and wished for. Imagine your inner child also now has a relationship with your tree that they can come to whenever they would have needed.

Notice how this feels in your body as you feel your own inner child supported. You can take your tree with you and time travel back into any moment of your life and be there as your adult self. Maybe practise on a few easier moments before tackling the most difficult.

Tree as Portal to Your Earth Cave

Your tree can help you have access to your own nourishing earth cave. This is a visualisation process. It is provided on audio in the ReRoot course, but you can read it through and do it on your own as well. You can do it on your next visit, or you can do it at home.

Imagine putting your roots down through your feet, to meet the earth, down they go, growing thicker and stronger as they go through the topsoil, through the clay, down through underwater streams and rock, down many kilometres down until they are so big and thick, they are the earth. Then they rest down deep, and you travel down them and pop out under the earth (your breathing body is always above so you don't have to worry about that). Ahead of you is a cave, it has your name on it.

Imagine you walk towards it and are standing in front of it. I want you to make it exactly how you want: the depth, the height, the colour, the lights, the comfort, what is in it. Put a place to lie down in it (I have a bed of feathers, in a small sanctuary of a cave, with fairy lights, candles, and soft music). Then go in and lie down in that cave and it is your cave of nourishment. Its purpose is to renew you and help you digest your life. Learn to breathe in the nourishment, the renewing energy, into all your trillions of cells; they all expand as you breathe this in, delighting in the life "givingness" of it. Breathe out tension, worries, anxieties, problems. Let your cells release what they have been holding or holding at bay. It is amazing to process life in a bigger body, the Earth's body. Do as many breaths as you wish. Then after a time, take at least ten more breaths exchanging your goodness, your essence with your cave. Then when you are ready, take your leave by thanking your cave and travelling back up your roots into your body. Notice how you feel. You can use this cave and your tree roots, accompanied by your own tree, any time you like. It is good to do as you go to sleep. We all need to digest our lives and renew each day.

Chapter 22
Deepening

In this section there are a range of different types of processes to try, all deepening the relatedness you are by now probably experiencing with some delight.

Ancestral Meetings

It may well be time for the ancestors to gather at your next meeting. Hopefully you have your own ritual of saying hello and goodbye now, and of attuning, really *meeting* your tree friend. In this next exercise, have the intent to connect both to your ancestors and the ancestors of the tree. This is hard to explain in our current dominant paradigm so maybe just do it first and see what happens. You are asking the ancestors to meet each other and hold a container in their realm for your relationship. Asking for help to open yourself to the relationship and to develop the sensitivity to relate, and for the tree to let you in. Feel into your own ancestral lines: first those on your mother's side and then your father's side. Feel where their place on this Earth was, where their connectivity was strongest. So much connectivity has been sliced, the tender tentacles cut off; see if you can have the intent to feel way back before this happened.

We all have indigenous roots into this beautiful planet, somewhere, even if it was long ago. For many in the western world these roots are completely severed. Where is that for you? Invoke those ancestors to help you reconnect as nature to nature, they know how. It has not gone. This is the start of restoration, with their help, with you. You may like to research an ancestor in both of your mother's and father's lines first. See who comes and bring them into this. Be aware that there is so much intergenerational trauma in all of our lines, and you may become conscious of this. In this exercise we are starting with the resilience and strength of these lines and those that are here to support you fully. Not all are.

Imagine your ancestors and the ancestors of the tree all meeting; maybe they even did. Trees are some of the most ancient beings on this planet. Feel the ancestral meeting as a meeting of creating a new future. The past comes into the present to create a new future. Imagine all who are part of this movement of building a global forest of humans and trees, together, all bringing their ancestors along with them, so we correct together the wrongs of the past and how we have treated this planet. Imagine they all gather around

I cannot, but together we all can.

your tree to start to weave a new relationship with Papatūānuku, *Mother Earth.*

What an inspiration this could be. I feel the ancestors also need to do their work to help heal the wrongs of the past. Together we create a weaving between past and present that rethreads our future.

Doing Absolutely Nothing

This could be the most difficult tree session you have, and I would encourage you to do this as often as you want. It is a session to come back to many times.

After you have arrived in your own ritualised way, just sit and do nothing. Absolutely nothing. Notice when you start to effort and come back to doing nothing. Be as much as possible in the returning to non-doing. Your mind will suggest many things you could do better; don't even do anything about that. It is a great practice of listening in the rhythm of silence and stillness. After you have done that for as long as you can bear, then you may want to map in some way your experience of navigating your own non-efforting.

Tree De-labelling

Labels are for jars a wise teacher once informed me. We love labels as humans and of course the visionary and detailed coding of trees into genus and species has helped us understand much. It can also distance us from a pure intimate meeting with life. Try taking all labels off your tree, and just experiencing it in a non-knowing way.

Imagine this is the first time you have met such a being and you have no idea what it is, just meet it being to being, experience it. Take all labels off as a defiant and powerful act of saying yes to intimacy. Yes to not knowing, yes to meeting with no barriers. Yes to the amazing act of life arising through two beings meeting each other. Feel you, the tree, and the space between you, the between. Be the experience itself of all of it. All of it arises in you.

Your Own Wise Elders Meeting

Imagine yourself twenty years from now being an accomplished tree whisperer. What qualities would you wish you had now? Let all your longing of what you wish you were arise. Imagine that your twenty-year older self has those qualities. They also are an able tree whisperer. They have learnt to be with their subtle body and receive communication from the natural world. Imbue those qualities in that older self. Then imagine they come behind you while you sit with your tree. They put their hands on your back and you rest back into them; they love you unconditionally as they know what it has taken for you to live your life. Then imagine as you rest back into those hands, all these qualities get transmitted into your being. Breathe them into all your cells: trillions of cells breathing in these qualities. Breathe in their ability to tree whisper; they will act as a living bridge for you. Ask for their help. This older self can be an ongoing wise guide for you in your life; you can ask them to come behind you whenever you need.

Feel your tree's qualities and imagine them transmitting into you. Imagine your tree in twenty years, how might it be different? Feel its own qualities becoming more powerful. Imagine these qualities also transmit into you. What does your noticing do with all this?

How do you feel?

Tree-streaming

Trees can help us access the future, now. Sit with your tree and ground with it; do your ritual of arriving and settling. Then when settled, put your focus on the top of your head, and imagine that the top of your head opens like a flower and the two hemispheres of your brain open a little. Then imagine that branches, beautiful branches, grow out of your head and your brain metres into the sky. Feel what they feel like at the top of those branches, with the leaves catching the light. Feel into that light, those leaves of you way up there. Notice all sensations through your body. Imagine you bring this light down into your body and into every cell. Just see what ideas or inspiration comes to you. It may be now; it may be later. See if you can feel any streaming, with this sensation is often a new flow of ideas. Let the words come. Write freely and see what comes and flows from your fingers! The longer you can hang out with the leaves of light, the more ideas may flow. Imagine a particular leaf of light slowly floats down your being all the way to your pelvis. Follow it with your inner sight. That leaf has something special for you. It may be an insight about your own purpose or next steps in your life. Hang out with the leaf and see if it is ready to give up its secrets. If not, leave it there to deliciously unfurl its wisdom for you in its own time.

Unseen Beings

Hopefully, by now you are tenderly suspicious of what you can see and what you cannot see, not confusing what you can see for all that there is. There are unseen beings around and in your tree, I know it. I have encountered them. *Just open your exquisite sensitivity to all your subtle layers* and ask them very respectfully if they would like to make contact. See what happens. Fairies and devas are often around trees and could be around yours. In *The Art of Mindful Gardening*, Ark Redwood, head gardener at Chalice Wells in Glastonberry, says these elementals represent the forces of nature. He says he doesn't quite see them but feels their energetic presence by what he calls a hush. I experience the same sense of "hushness" that gives you an indication more is there. So open to this hushness and the felt sense of any magic afoot. Many people take plant medicine for experiencing this. I know we can also learn to become so sensitised with our own practices that our eyes open beyond our mind.

The unseen ones may take a while to trust you so I would give this plenty of time, space, and opening.

Recovering Your Own Photosynthesising Self

This is a beautiful and deep process that may take you some years of practice. That, however, always starts one practice at a time and we build up muscle for it. Trees are transformers of energy, and so are we, or we can be. We have the ability to transmute the past trauma into free energy.

When next at your tree, stand and feel into your own treeness. Stand with it, with your roots well into the ground, and your branches, your arms, and upper body heading toward the sky. Feel back into the tree-streaming exercise, allowing yourself to expand up to reach the light. Imagine that light streaming down your whole body. Now feel into something happening in the world you wish were not so (there is plenty to choose from!) or something in your own experience that has not been healthy. See how this lands in your body. Present it to yourself; bring it into your belly or heart and then feel the light streaming down to meet it.

It is often a dense feeling when we sense traumas from the past; let this be there and then feel it being woven and infused with light. We can always transform past or lesser or shadow energies into lighter, more flowing, vital energies. Just experiment with this in small bits, titrated experiences, that we thread light into like a light dance. It is your own process of photosynthesising.

See if you can catch the movement of life in a creative way. Your tree and you both have and are light beings. See if you can look at your tree in that way, receive it as a being of light, and then turn back and see into yourself in this way. What would it be like to move forward, walk, breathe, sing from that?

You as Braided River

On your next visit, stand with your tree and invoke support for letting go of anything you have known to be real. The way I experience it, even our bodies are not a thing. They are fluid and movement, and many layers are always communicating with the environment beyond our level of consciousness. Feel the layers of yourself, a many-layered being communing with the natural world around you, layers of bacteria, layers of fungi in us communicating with those layers in the so-called outside. We are a confluence, an assemblage, as thought leader and activist Bayo Akomalefe puts it. I feel this; see if you can, and just imagine all your body systems communicating with the environment around you. What can you imagine is happening? What might you be aware of that is actually happening?

I love the twoness becoming one.

Feel these layers of you communing with the layers in your tree. There are so many layers in both of you; see what you become aware of, what part of your body. What body system and what is it tuning into in your tree? This process helps us weave and become aware of the many layers to the connective tissue between us and other beings.

Catching the Current

This is such a beautiful capacity to cultivate and is simple.

Stand near your tree and receive the tree with your whole body. Receive all its gifts and its presence that you have learnt to be in relationship with, open to receive its essence, breathe it in. Then feel into this current and give your own goodness and joy back. Let your delight catch the current and delight in it, sending your goodness, your essence, into that current. Your presence.

Appreciate its beauty; inhale its full gift to you and reflect yours back. You are nourished and nature is nourished by you.

This sounds simple, and yet is a profound exchange. It is a profound current for you to start to feel and connect with and orientate your life to.

This is a good one to dance to, to feel that current, move your body, do your own little jig or flow that the movement feels as you catch it.

Becoming Polyamorous

Okay, so now it is time to get to know other trees, so you can feel the difference between them. It also helps deepen your many relationships. You will know when it is time, as another tree will be catching your attention, wanting to commune with you. Is that happening? Or you may just feel the tug, but not know yet which one. I would recommend going back to the first exercise of taking yourself out and seeing which one chooses you now. I won't repeat the whole exercise but go back and read it and start to expand your forest of human-tree connectivity. You are now starting to create your own mini forest, your own web of trees. This is your own circle of tree beings.

See if a different tree, a different type and energy, is calling you. At the beginning of our journey, I introduced you to some of mine, flowering cherry, lemon myrtle, Pōhutukawa, all so different in their frequency and medicine.

I love imagining you doing this, and I feel so excited for you as you find a new friend.

And how cool that you get to play out your polyamorous self!

Go On Then, Give It a Hug

I specifically avoided *tree hugging* at the beginning. I didn't want this to be labelled a tree-huggers journey without all the hard work required to feel the tree hug, to really hug the tree, and maybe even to feel it hug you back, in a tree way.

I have seen tree auras. I have wondered if it is the tree's way of hugging me, of enfolding me in them and their energy. I certainly feel like this when I can see it, and, I must admit, I have also felt like this when I haven't seen it, so I think it is more about my own seeing ability at given times.

See if you can feel it, and feel it as the tree's way of hugging, of embracing you.

Chapter 23
Going Even Deeper

This section of exercises and processes enable us to go much deeper so don't put pressure on yourself to do them. You may want to just cycle back to the start or to the ones you like or to creating your own.

If you do want to try these, then again, please go playfully, just seeing what happens. Pressure reduces our awareness and contracts our body system and then we often only experience our stories by mentalising and nothing else.

Remember always ask yourself, what is it I am feeling, sensing? What am I noticing? Do not focus on what is *not* happening.

Remember also that feeling nothing, blank and numb, is a feeling, and if we can allow that, presence that, a lot can arise in that place.

Foresting

Forest bathing is a beautiful movement in the world and worth exploring. I know not everyone has easy access to a forest and I have tried to make this book equitable for all people to do within walking distance whether in a city or in the country. But forests are superb so if you can, please go. Even small forests. You know how to enter these with reverence and just to bathe in the presence of all the trees together. I would encourage you to just sit somewhere with your spine against a tree and allow all that magnificence to enter you, until you feel your own being become part of that forest system for the time you are there. There are known networks under the ground as has been outlined but I believe and sometimes see the webs of energy that connect the trees above the ground. You can sit still, and they will connect through you, and you will be part of this connection. It is healing, it is vital, it is nourishing, it is magical. Hang out for as long as you can and experience your own forest self.

Collapsing Distance

We often see ourselves and anything else as separate entities and there is a distance between. This is a wonderful practice. See if you can practise "collapsing distance." You are looking at your tree as though you are two separate beings. *Imagine the distance between you collapses. There is no space. There is no between.* This is quite trippy, but I love it so much. What do you notice as you collapse the distance between you and your tree?

I love how twoness becomes one.

Tree Eroticism

One of the most beautiful experiences in my life was when I was able to slide into the tree body, inhabit it, feel it from the inside. It was such an erotic and enlivening process. Like everything, a natural principle throughout all of life, you need consent. You need an invitation and readiness. Ask your tree for her consent. Sit next to it and see if you can collapse the distance between you and your tree in your awareness. Distance is something we do, as a process. It isn't a thing. Then use your imagination because imagination always opens doors and portals to what our rational brain may crush with facts. Don't try too hard; see what happens as you imagine going inside the tree, assuming it gave you permission!

You can lie down and relax and feel the rhythm of the earth and tree roots and see if that rhythm can take you inside. Keep imagining, keep imagining. Keep relaxing, breathing, asking, collapsing distance. It will either happen or it won't happen yet. Don't fret; it is something to keep practising.

Once you can do this, the world of nature opens like a great flowering. You can ride the wind or fly with a bird, but that is another book!

Just give it a go. It takes time, patience, and a melting of who we think we are.

We meet our spirit, we meet the spirit of the tree, we are let inside to feel her and be with her in an entirely different world.

Totality of Being

You may well experience now that this relationship with your tree is requiring you to have a greater relationship with the totality of your being including your earth self, space self, light self, no self, hurt self, true self. You may notice that the inside and outside don't feel so different, that there is a merging of these. Sometimes I am walking and feel I am walking inside myself through the trees, valleys, and paths. It is all inside me, and sometimes I feel inside the trees, valleys, and paths. Play with this next time you visit your tree. See if you can open your own perception to experiment with inside/outside. They are not what they may seem.

Experiencing the Unity Already There

When you feel into your tree, when you see your tree, they are arising in your perception, so they are arising in you. See if you can grow your own sense of the field around you. *There are layers to the space you take up in the universe: your node, your place, your space goes further than your own body. Imagine the tree is now in that field of you; in that place there is interbeing. There is a connective tissue that involves your body but also involves your own energetic field.*

This is more a mystery practice but give it a go and it helps to move beyond our familiar sense of self, which is always too limited. You are a vast being engaging with a vast being, exchanging breath. Layers of your body system are in communion with your tree without you even realising it.

See whatever you encounter when you do this deep exercise, just sitting and communing, seeing what sensations arise in your body.

The Tree Sensing You

This is outrageous! Trees sensing us? How could this be? How could it *not* be? You know you are paradigm switching when this makes sense to you, you have gone into the web of life!

Next time at your tree, or during any of the other processes, feel your sensing of yourself, then your sensing of your tree, then see if you can feel it sensing you.

I am going to leave that there, like a *koan*. This is your discovery of what you find. It is amazing when you can feel the tendrils of the tree, the energy field, sensing you and making adjustments for what it senses.

Tree Fixing

You may by now feel like you have a good handle on your tree and that you are getting to know it.

This process invites you to give up all knowing you have accumulated. Trees, like us, arrive out of the boundlessness of life itself, and they are always arriving. We easily concretise them as we do people and everything else, putting all into a category, and then we relate to the category or our image of the thing, rather than the thing or person itself.

During your next encounter, take off all you have learnt and see if you can let the tree arrive in you afresh. We are going to take the tree out of any boxes you may have put her in.

It is difficult to discard everything we have learnt, so don't try too hard. Invite them to arrive afresh, imagine your mind opening at the top of your head to the sky, so your mind and sky become one and all categorising and fixing of your tree as a certain thing just floats off.

See what you notice afresh. You could let yourself arise afresh also. What would it be like to take all judgements and assessments off yourself? You are arriving here right now, tree whispering. Who knew!

What Arrives?

What if your tree is actually a process, a movement of life, not an object? It is really "treeing." Can you relate to it as a movement, an expression in life, of life?

What would it be to relate to yourself in this way? You are "humaning" not an object either, a verb, a movement. Can you be two movements moving together?

Feel into the movement of you, the quality that you are not a firm object, that you are a movement, an arc through life. Just feel yourself this way. Then when you have a sense of your own fluidity, look at your tree and see if you can see it also as a fluid movement. Look at how it has moved and grown throughout the years and how this movement is all captured and that it is still moving and growing.

This all sounds more esoteric I know, but let's just go there for now. See what happens if you don't fix yourself or your tree as a thing, but can feel the fluidity of both, the continual moving and growing of you both.

How does that change your relating between you and your tree? It may be a bit disorientating but see if you can let yourself be disorientated. It can deliver new insights, awakenings, and the felt sense of life can alter as we do this. How might you creatively express this disorientation? Creativity has deeper ways of expressing these depths without having to make sense of them which often disrupts the potent rewiring trying to happen. Movement is good here too; just move your body as you feel moved and as you feel yourself as a movement.

Tree Space

We are going to focus this exercise on the space around and through the tree. We are going to foreground space. We have been focusing on the form of tree.

This exercise is great for drawing, drawing the space around and in the tree, rather than the tree.

You can do that as you arrive to see what happens.

Then sit back and really start noticing the space between you and the tree, around the tree, through the branches, way up to the sky, behind you. We perceive the space as empty, but it isn't. Imagine or feel now that it is full of alive presence and energy. I often see energy and the energy around trees is amazing, there is so much happening. For now, just feel into it as a substance. When you move, you alter that substance.

Movement is also good here; move as though you are drawing with your body into that space. What does it feel like to dance and move in space with consciousness? You are dancing in the space between you and the tree.

Do another drawing when you have finished. What do you notice about the space now? Try not to be too literal in your drawing, just see what shows up. How does your picture look different from the first one?

Enjoy the space that you and your tree have created. You have sewn connective tissue in that space that will now never go away, no matter how far away from your tree you go.

Feel the space that is always around you, in you. Space also arises within us.

Enjoy what you have created.

Honour the effort you have put in to get here.

Deeply bow to yourself and your tree.

Remattering

We are always "mattering." Our matter is moving, reconfiguring, changing, dancing. I enjoy consciously putting my attention on my mattering process. It is like tapping into the creative current of life in all my cells. We also need to matter to ourselves to feel our mattering.

Next time you are at your tree, slowly feel into the layers of systems in your body. Your bones, muscles, circulatory system, endocrine, organs, skin, all the parts of you, and give them full permission to "rematter," to reconfigure to now reflect more the earth consciousness you have been embodying through this journey. Imagine they all upgrade to become coherent as a new version of you.

Imagine this version of yourself and your tree come into relationship in a new depth, and we all "matter" together. You are both forming, constantly arising as form from this current of life. Enjoy yourself again as a process, and enjoy your tree as a process, both giving expression to life in your own unique ways with your own unique medicine.

Magnificence

How are you feeling right now? I am hoping if you are reading this you have become more deeply connected with your tree and with the natural flow of life.

I also hope you have discovered that this process was also about realising your own magnificence. Humans have not been magnificent. Let's face it. And that does not mean that we are not. Trauma energy has been driving humans for many centuries.

Do you get a sense of your own magnificence, your own radiance? If you are earth, you must be magnificent too. We all can embody Mother Earth consciousness, and in fact, we need enough of us to do that to catch the evolutionary natural current of life and get out of the fear currents.

This journey has been about embodying that consciousness, so we come from that into our relationship with ourselves, others, and the immensity of the beauty this living planet truly is.

Take a moment now to embody that more. Feel you can expand into your rightful place in life, where you fully bring your magnificence and medicine. Not from the ego, but from your essential being that truly belongs and has a place. If we all found our place, we could become that orchestra as the humanity that we need, and we would allow all species to take their place as well, and we would start undoing and transforming those threads of superiority that led us so astray.

Write a poem, song, or chant about your own radiance, to capture its essence, and when you next visit your tree,

Magnificence meeting magnificence to create magnificence.

take that magnificence to the magnificence of your tree being, two beings arising from Mother Earth meeting each other in mutual love. Greet your tree in your way from this place. Touch it from this place and let yourself be touched from this place of your tree. This is what pure love feels like.

Chapter 24
The Journey
Without an End

I cannot bring myself to write a conclusion as there really isn't one. It is a movement that needs to continue well into the future.

Imagine if we all could connect in this way, to ourselves, back into the web of life, and with others from this felt and layered relation with the world. What would it mean for our solutions and the way we approach our systems to change and create our new world? I think it would be radically different in flow, essential, connected, radical collaboration. How can we all be the system changing rather than waiting for or demanding the system change? How does our own system become so coherent that it is a system that harmonises the world around us?

Human superiority, like white superiority, has had its day, and it is time we changed that.

How might this work of reconnection to and as Earth affect our work together in being a system changing? Imagine if we all inhabited the paradigm of equal people and equal beings. We were all equally allowed to thrive and have our place in the wholeness we all live in.

From this paradigm of connectivity, imagine that we then created our systems, structures, processes, policies, legislation. We became like the caring underground mycorrhizal network of the trees. We became part of this, and everything was created from it.

We have a connectivity crisis, and the only way back is to do this rethreading, and if I do mine and you yours and us ours, we will create a radical shift in the world.

This is a process of restoration, of sewing, of threading ourselves back into the connectivity that is always there and redesigning from that.

You are now well on the way. If you have even done half of this journey, you are on your way. I hope in the journey of befriending your tree, romancing a tree, you have "reromanced" yourself, reconfigured who you are, re-enchanted yourself and who you think you are. In meeting your tree in so many layers of depth, I hope you have met yourself in your many layers, a mystery unfolding. I hope you can feel your source connection and how your own connection with the flow of life is now more open to you. I hope you love your tree. I hope you can feel its love for you. I hope you feel more rooted in yourself and with the earth. I hope you have felt us on this journey with you, including you and your tree, into our human-tree forest around the world.

This building of the global human-tree forest is continuing; it won't stop. The stronger the sewing the stronger the nest, the stronger the nest, the more potential we unlock together. Let's watch and see what is unfolding as this type of pure connection makes magic happen.

By all means, stay in any way an environmental activist, but also become an environmental relationist. This is the essence of the book, that this relationship combined with our action is vital for all beings to thrive on this beautiful planet.

As you can understand it is not the work of trees to do—they are already connected beings—it is the work of humans to do.

There are so many more things you can do with your tree, just as you can with any relationship. Many of the above you can do again and again. You will now know your own way of experiencing this relationship because you are now an earth being, a walking tree. You will have discovered your own treeness—your own grounded and interwoven self.

Ko te rākau ko aue

Ko aue ko te rākau

I am the tree; the tree is me.

I will let you in on a secret. Mostly I communed with my trees on this book, but not always. Some of the knowledge didn't come from the trees, it came from the sea, the *moana*. She whispered from her fluid body to mine, one fluid body full of potent ideas. Any part of nature we connect to, connects us to every part. So, it doesn't finish here. Which part of nature calls you to come closer? You can use many of these processes with any part of the web of life.

You can also share with others. How about starting a tree circle and doing the journey together with friends, family, work colleagues, especially if you work with the environment? See what happens close to home, in a group, as you all reroot yourselves.

Unlocking the potential of groups is a passion and longtime experiment of mine, to weave the interbeing threads together. I know it creates fields of coherence in groups or "we-spaces" that heal, transform, and generate.

I know doing this journey with you has changed me. I didn't realise how much more slowing was needed in my own system to go to another level of rerooting. I join this movement also with my tree friends, always evolving and growing me.

Thank you to each one of you for your company. I could feel you gathering as I wrote this. I deeply bow to you all.

And the final words from one of my trees:

You may not yet see or feel the mycel we have created, the network of fibres that builds our nest, but trust us in the energetic world, the magic has begun.

Glossary of Terms

*indicates a non-*Māori* word

Aotearoa–the original *Māori* name for New Zealand.

Atua–a deity, sacred being, or god.

Hongi–to press noses in greeting, breathing the essence of each other through touching foreheads and noses.

Kāinga–home, residence.

Kaitiaki–guardians.

Koan*–a riddle used in Zen Buddhism to provoke enlightenment.

Korero–a conversation.

Mahi–work, practice, activity, a sense of sacred work.

Maunga–mountain.

Mauri–life principle, life force, vital essence, special nature, a material symbol of a life principle, the essential quality and vitality of a being or entity; also used for a physical object, individual, ecosystem, or social group in which this essence is located.

Mauri tau–relaxation, calmness.

Moana–the ocean.

Ngahere–forests.

Ngāi Tūhoe–a *Māori* tribe in New Zealand, often called *Children of the Mist*.

Pachamama*–in Incan mythology she is an "Earth Mother" type goddess.

Papatūānuku–Earth, Earth Mother, and wife of *Ranginui*.

Patupaiarehe–fairy, mystical small being now in the invisible realms to most.

Pōhutukawa–a large and beautiful coastal tree that flowers in red blooms in the summer.

Qigong*–moving meditation with origins in ancient China.

Rangatira–to be of high rank, become of high rank, entailed, esteemed, revered.

Ranginui–*atua* of the sky and husband of *Papatūānuku* from which union originate all living things.

Rākau–a tree, stick, timber, wood, spar, mast.

Rongoā–to treat, apply medicines, or inherent medicine itself.

Te Reo Māori–the *Māori* language.

Te Urewera–the tribal area of *Ngai Tūhoe* in New Zealand.

Waiata–song.

Wairua–spirit, soul; spirit of a person which exists beyond death; it is the non-physical spirit, distinct from the body and the *mauri*.

Whare–house, building, residence, dwelling.

Whenua–land, country, nation; also the name for placenta.

Whāriki–woven mat.

Resources

Tree science–wonderful research on tree beings

- Craig Holdrege, (2013), *Thinking Like a Plant: A Living Science for Life*, SteinerBooks.

- Peter Wohlleben, (2016), *The Hidden Life of Trees*, Black Incorporated.

- Robin Wall Kimmerer, (2020), *Braiding Sweetgrass: Indigenous Wisdom, Scientific Knowledge and the Teaching of Plants*, Penguin Books Limited.

- Stefano Mancuso, Alessandra Viola, (2015), *Brilliant Green: The Surprising History and Science of Plant Intelligence*, Island Press.

- Susan Simard, (2021), *Finding the Mother Tree: Uncovering the Wisdom and Intelligence of the Forest*, Penguin UK.

Inspirational nature connection and connected worldview books

- Ark Redwood, (2018), *The Art of Mindful Gardening: Sowing the Seeds of Meditation*, Leaping Hare Press.

- Catriona MacGregor, (2010), *Partnering with Nature: The Wild Path to Reconnecting with the Earth*, Beyond Words Publishing.

- Gary Snyder, (2020), *The Practice of the Wild*, Counterpoint Press.

- Joanna Macy, (2007), *World as Lover, World as Self: Courage for Global Justice and Ecological Renewal*, Parallax Press.

- John Seed, Joanna Macy, Pat Fleming, Arne Naess, (1988), *Thinking Like a Mountain: Towards a Council of All Beings*, New Society Publishers.
- Malidoma Patrice Somé, (1994), *Of Water and Spirit*, Penguin Publishing Group.

Nature connecting poetry and spirituality

- Mary Oliver, (2017), *Devotions: The Selected Poems by Mary Oliver*, Penguin Publishing Group.
- Stephen Mitchell, (2006), *Tao Te Ching*, HarperCollins Publishers.

Journalling

- Julia Cameron, (2002), *Walking in this World*, Random House.
- Linda Trichter, (2008), *Writing the Mind Alive: The Proprioceptive Method for Finding your Authentic Voice*, Random House Publishing Group.

Somatic experiencing, the nervous system, and trauma

- Peter A. Levine, PhD, (2010), *In an Unspoken Voice: How the Body Releases Trauma and Restores Goodness*, North Atlantic Books.
- Stephen W. Porges (2011), *The Polyvagal Theory: Neurophysiological Foundations of Emotions, Attachment, Communication, and Self-regulation* (Norton Series on Interpersonal Neurobiology). 1st Edition. W. W. Norton & Company.
- Thomas Hubl (2020), *Healing Collective Trauma: A Process for Integrating Our Intergenerational and Cultural Wounds*, Sounds True and MacMillian Publishing.

Poetry

All works of these poets are beautiful to read and so helpful to reconnect to nature.

Alexis Pauline Gumbs

Camille T. Dungy

David Whyte

Gary Snyder

Helene Johnson

Hone Tuwhare

Dr Karlo Mila

Lucille Clifton

Malidoma Somé

Mary Oliver

Robert Bly

Robert Frost

Wendell Berry

A Call to Action

Join into the movement, ReRoot

www.reroot.world

Via a self-paced programme that helps guide you through the reconnective journey with audio, videos, and a workbook, plus the work supports the creation of planted corridors.

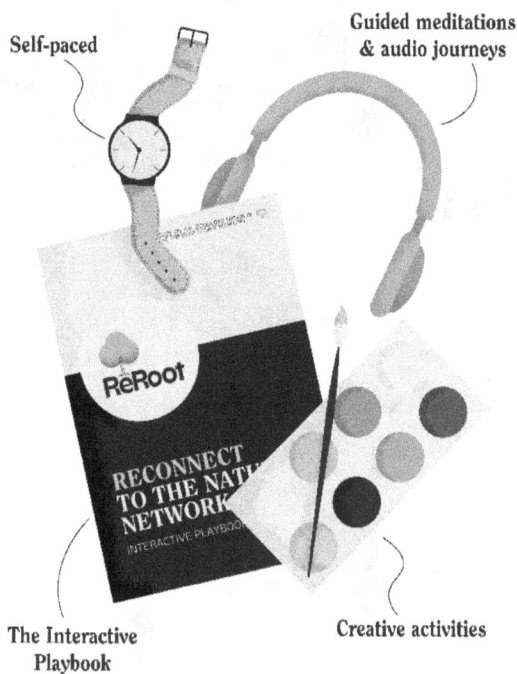

Self-paced

Guided meditations & audio journeys

The Interactive Playbook

Creative activities

You can also join the community of other nature networkers and receive updates and free Q and A calls with Louise.

You can check out Louise's other work at Unity House:

www.unityhouse.nz

Make sure to follow us on Instagram and Facebook as @reroot.world for more on how you can form an empowering reconnection with nature and grow a life-changing relationship with a tree. We love to hear your stories and see your photos, don't forget to tag us on your journey!

About the Author

Louise Marra works in the healing of systems, organisations, communities, and individuals. Her unique blend of understanding, experience, and education in both the nature of self and systems has led her to global work and also in Aotearoa, New Zealand. Locally, Louise works on deep and restorative systems change around major issues of the time such as colonisation and climate challenges from both collective and individual layers. Her leadership experience has spanned all sectors having held senior leadership roles within government, the private sector, philanthropy, and the NGO sector. She has been an adviser to the Prime Minister, director of a company, led a collaborative government office, and has aided in the set-up of social innovation labs both for government and for philanthropy. Louise's passion is to help build the next era of conscious leaders, innovators, activists, and organisations robust enough to enable radical innovation for an emergent and evolutionary approach to personal, social, and environmental change. She has studied individual, collective, and intergenerational trauma for many years and now runs her own company, Unity House, and is a founder of the social enterprise ReRoot, aimed at nature reconnection.